B. Chirva

SOCCER
Training the «game episodes technique», beginning from coming over the ball in open play

2017

УДК 796 332
Ч 64

Ч 64 **Chirva B.** Soccer. Training the «game episodes technique», beginning from coming over the ball in open play. – Moscow, 2017. – 220 p.

ISBN 978-5-98724-197-4

Method of perfection of the «game episodes technique», beginning from coming over the ball in open play, by players is represented.

This method is developed on the basis of the regularities of soccer, specificity in performing techniques in different areas of the pitch and transition of fitness in speed and precision of actions with the ball.

Sets of exercises for training the «game episodes technique» in the 18-yard box, in attacking, midfield and defensive zones.

Materials are designed for coaches working in professional soccer teams and youth soccer.

УДК 796 332
Ч 64

ISBN 978-5-98724-197-4

© Chirva B., «ТВТ Дивизион», 2017

All rights reserved

CONTENTS

Introduction..6
The symbols...8

Chapter 1. Constructing drills
for perfection of «game episodes
technique»...10

Chapter 2. General description of drills
for perfection of «game episodes
technique», beginning after
over the ball in open play.........................14

Chapter 3. Perfection of «game episodes
Technique» in the 18-yard box..................18
Characteristics of constructing drills..........18
Training the game technique while finishing
the attacking actions with a foot kick........25
    Drills with a regular beginning
    and regular finishing of players'
    of actions with the ball..........................25
    Drills with a regular beginning
    and variative finishing of players'
    of actions with the ball..........................43
    Drills with a variative beginning
    and variative finishing of players'
    of actions with the ball..........................60
Training the game technique while finishing
the attacking actions with a header..........90
    Drills with a regular beginning
    and regular finishing of players'
    of actions with the ball..........................93

Drills with a regular beginning
and variative finishing of players'
of actions with the ball……..………………....….....101
Drills with a variative beginning
and variative finishing of players'
of actions with the ball……..……...…………....……107

Chapter 4. Perfection of «game episodes technique» in the attacking zone……..……………….......112
Characteristics of the drills construction………....……......112
Drills in which the ball is delivered
into the 18-yard box by means of dribbling…...………….. 117
Drills in which the ball is delivered
into the 18-yard box by means of a pass……..…………….132
Drills in which the ball is delivered
into the 18-yard box by means of
combination of dribbling and passes……..………....……..146
Drills in which shots on goal from
the outside of the 18-yard box are performed…….…......... 160

Chapter 5. Perfection of «game episodes technique» in the middle and defensive zones……....……174
Characteristics of constructing drills…….…….................174
Drills in which space is covered
by means of dribbling…………….....………….....……177
Drills in which space is covered by means
of passes with a second touch, performed
immediately after the first touch……………….....……….. 185
Drills in which space is covered
by means of combination of dribbling
and short and medium passes……..………….....……..191
Drills in which space is covered
by means of passes at a long distance……….………….205

Afterword……..………………………………..….214
Bibliography……..…………………………….......216

Soccer. Training the «game episodes technique», beginning from coming over the ball in open play

For notes

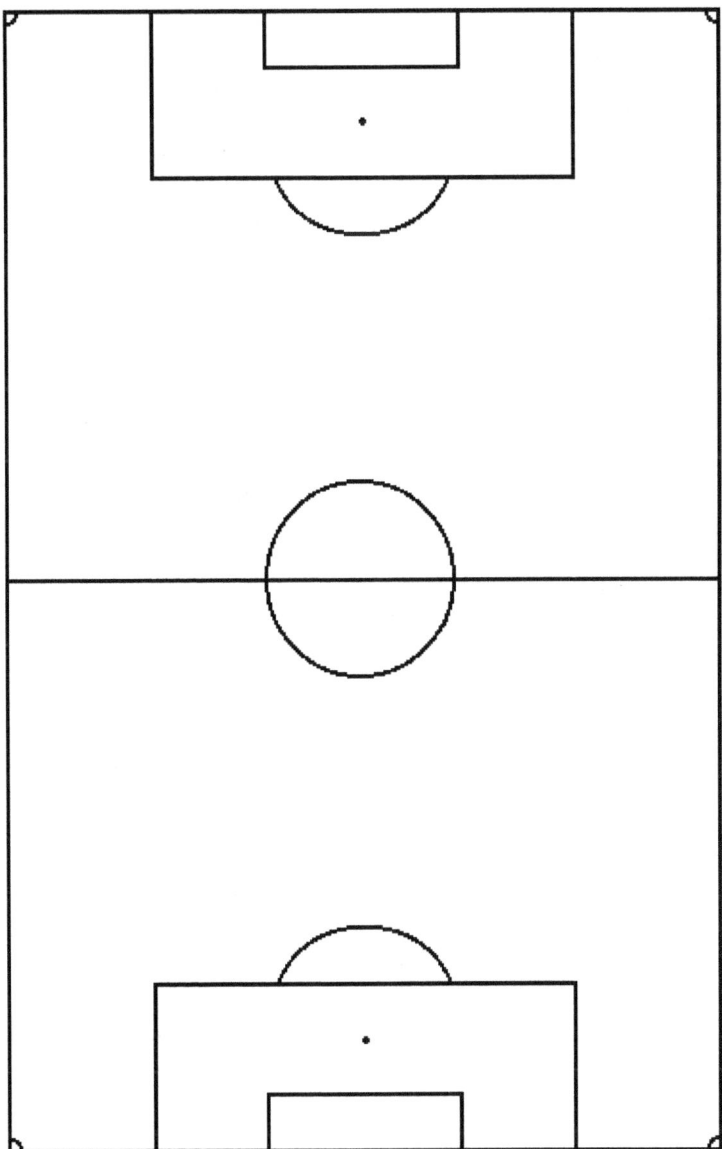

INTRODUCTION

Whereas it is the most important for players to learn the structure of movements while learning techniques, the main task in perfection of the «game episodes technique» is to adapt technical skills, learned earlier, to conditions of competitive games. This task may be solved in case players would actually train the «game episodes technique», obligingly performing a large amount of actions with the ball.

There are three stages that may be marked out in any attack, resulting in shooting on goal: the beginning, the evolvement and the finishing. Therefore game episodes, during which players try to score a goal, may be classified by common features depending on:
 – how it begins: with players coming over the ball that is already «in play» (as a result of an interception or a tackle after a pass from a partner), or with putting the ball into play after a break (with performing penalties, corners, free kicks, throw-ins);
 – where it begins and evolves (in the defensive, middle or attacking zone);
 – where it finishes (in the opponent's 18-yard box or beyond it).

Players' decision taking on actions with the ball and technical performance of techniques on each stage of an attack and when passing from one stage of an attack to another in competitive matches happen with some particularities, which are defined by the conditions and point of actions with the ball.

In this regard the same specific characteristics of taking decisions about actions with the ball and technical performance of techniques in different areas of the pitch should take place in drills for perfection of «game episodes technique».

There are various situations occurring in competitive matches that may repeat less or more often and differ in the context of an amount of contribution of players' successful actions in these situations into the outcome of a match.

In fact, there may be all shades of opinion regarding what may secure a victory in a match and, subsequently, what should be occupied more or less in trainings. Regardless of subjective perceptions of soccer, though, game episodes which properly define the result exist objectively.

Obviously, these game episodes should be paid with a particular attention in the training work from the respective of both perfecting of technical skill and exercising the tactics of actions. First of all it concerns the attacking and defensive actions in the 18-yard box.

Method of perfection of the «game episodes technique» in various areas of the pitch, beginning from coming over the ball in open play, by footballers is represented in this book.

THE SYMBOLS

Legend keys presented in fig. 1 below are used in describing exercises and goalkeepers and footballers' actions in this book.

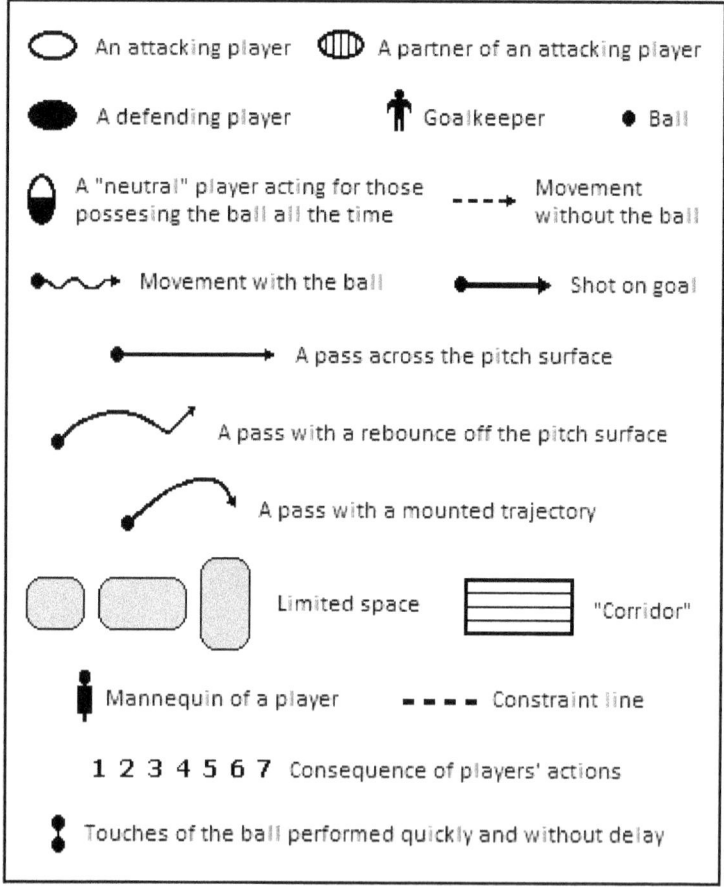

Fig. 1. Legend keys used in describing exercises and footballers' actions

Soccer. Training the «game episodes technique», beginning from coming over the ball in open play

For notes

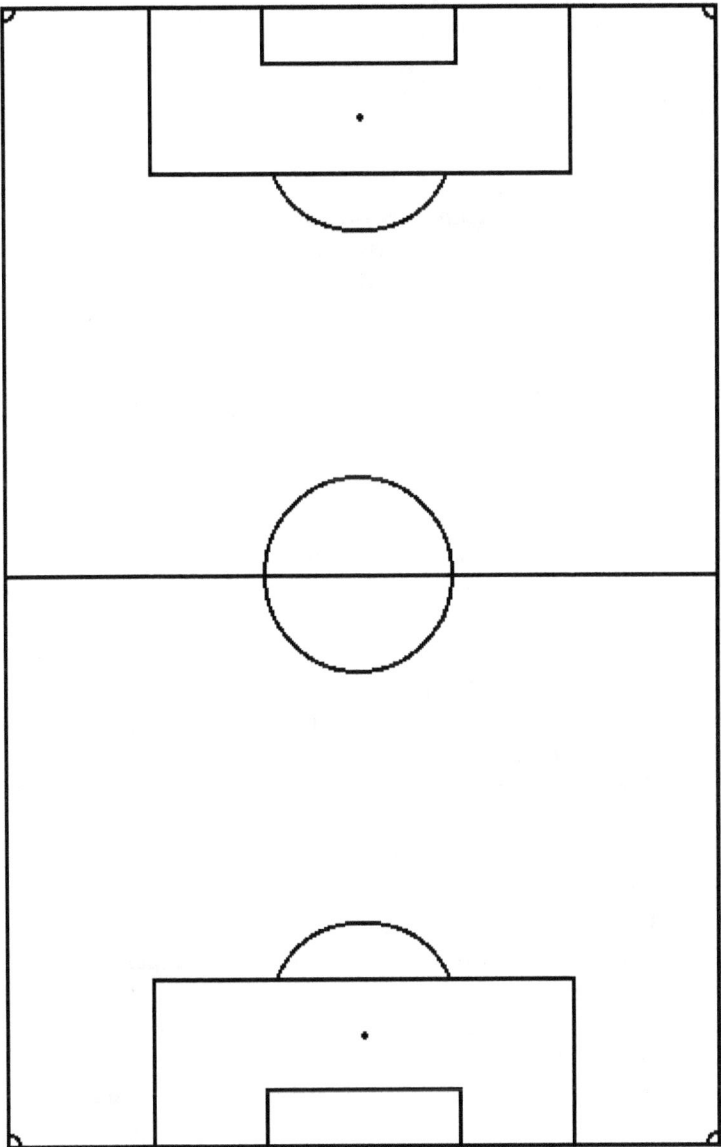

CHAPTER 1.
CONSTRUCTING DRILLS FOR PERFECTION OF «GAME EPISODES TECHNIQUE»

In some sport games (court and paddle tennis, basketball, handball, volleyball) the sportsman's technical skill is largely improved directly during competitions, as the large amount of players' contacts with the ball in competitive matches is the most favorable for improving the technique of possession.

Such is the specificity of soccer that players cannot handle the ball too often in competitive matches, and thus training drills in soccer are crucial as in no other kind of sport games.

While organizing drills with the ball they often apply common sense: if players shoot on goal, move with the ball and pass it to each other, then it seems that the technique of possession is bound to be trained in such drill.

Sure enough, not every interaction with the ball may be considered soccer, and not everything that is performed with the ball by feet and head allow players to improve their skill in handling the ball, necessary for playing soccer.

Therefore some drills with the ball may correspond the real soccer and help towards the growth of the players' technical skill, whereas other are virtually just an «entertainment with the ball».

It is necessary to «train soccer» to play soccer, and so the focal point of skilled players' work while perfecting the technical prowess represents a training of a technique of actions with the ball, specific for various areas of the pitch, – the «game episodes technique».

Setting two main objectives – delivering the ball to the shooting position and goalscoring – is the key for constructing drills for perfecting «game episodes technique».

While developing these drills it is to consider:
- soccer regularities (of statistical character) reflecting display of the technical prowess by players while delivering the ball to the shooting position and goalscoring;
- specificity in the technique of actions with the ball in definite episodes of competitive matches;
- regularities of the transition of fitness in quickness and precision of actions with the ball (fig. 2).

In case of disregard of one of three mentioned provisions the efficiency of drills for perfecting the technical prowess by skilled players reduces drastically, while it is next to nothing in case all three are ignored.

Distinctive features of modern soccer technique are players' abilities to perform actions with the ball:
- with stepping kicking motions;
- displaying a maximum power of actions;
- with a physical contact with an opponent;
- back to an opponent (to the opponent's goal);
- with a head.

To achieve the transition of fitness in quickness and precision of actions with the ball while moving from training drills to conditions of competitive games, the organization of drills with the ball should provide the observance of two main principles:
- coincidence of conditions of drills performance with those of one or another episode of competitive matches on kinematic and dynamic characteristics of performance of actions with the ball;
- possibility for players to perform a large amount of actions with the ball in specialized conditions.

As far as actions with the ball in competitive games are performed in three quite clearly distinguished zones of power emergence (low and medium, high, maximal), players have to train techniques with demonstration of relevant power of actions.

It is very important that leg muscles are also in the same condition they are in competitive matches, i.e. unspecialized load of a local nature on leg muscles should be excluded.

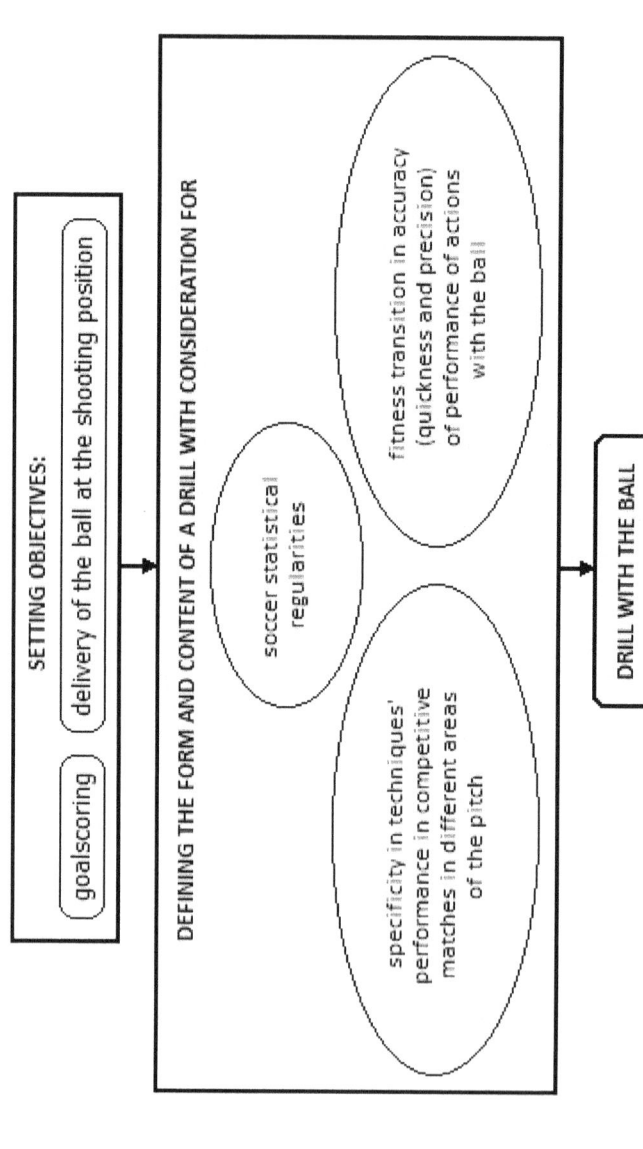

Fig. 2. Algorithm of constructing drills for perfection of the «game episodes technique» by players

Considering that each player handles the ball not so often in competitive matches, there is the only way for players to gain a large amount of repeats of various actions with the ball in specialized conditions – multiply repeat actions with the ball which simulate those that are performed in particular episodes of competitive matches.

It is hard enough to specify the minimum of repeats of one or another actions with the ball in a certain drill that results in improvement of its performance in competitive matches, as far as it depends both on complexity of action and players' qualification.

As researches of the transition of fitness in quickness and precision of actions with the ball have shown, this minimum is 25-30 repeats of a certain action with the ball on average with a necessary quality in a certain drill.

The higher the level of players' displaying the quickness and precision in actions with the ball, the more repeats of these actions are required for its increasing.

CHAPTER 2.
GENERAL DESCRIPTION OF DRILLS FOR PERFECTION OF THE «GAME EPISODES TECHNIQUE», BEGINNING FROM COMING OVER THE BALL IN OPEN PLAY

On grounds of the analysis of condition and specificity in performance of actions with the ball by outfield players in competitive matches in various areas of the pitch defined are three kinds of the «game episodes technique» and subsequently developed are three groups of drills for perfection of the «game episodes technique», beginning from coming over the ball that is already in open play, by players.

The first group of drills consists of tasks for improving the technique of play in the 18-yard box. Statistical regularities of goalscoring with a foot and head from the 18-yard box and specific characteristics of techniques performance in this area of the pitch were considered while constructing them.

Second and third groups consist of tasks for training of the «game episodes technique» in the attacking zone (no further than 35 meters from the defending team's goal-line) and in defensive and middle zones (no closer than 35 meters from the defending team's goal-line) subsequently. These drills were developed with due consideration of statistical regularities of goalscoring attacks and specificity in performance of actions with the ball in various areas of the pitch.

In various conditions of competitive matches players may act:

– deliberately, when they know what they would do in advance;

– deliberately or on impulse, when one variant of actions is selected of two or three possible ones depending on the scenario on the pitch;

– on impulse.

Considering that the techniques performance may vary depending on how the making decision on actions is going on, there should be various degree of premeditation and improvisation of players' actions in drills for perfection of the «game episodes technique», beginning from coming over the ball in open play.

Taking this into account, there are three kinds of drills, in which players' actions with the ball subsequently:
– begin and finish regularly;
– begin regularly and finish variatively;
– begin and finish variatively (see the table).

Classification of drills for perfection of the «game episodes technique» in various areas of the pitch, beginning from coming over the ball in open play

Drills for perfection of the «game episodes technique»		
In the 18-yard box	In the attacking zone	In the middle and defensive zones
Beginning and finishing regularly		
Beginning regularly and finishing variatively		
Beginning and finishing variatively		

In drills with a regular beginning and regular or variative finishing of actions with the ball the point of their beginning and finishing, and also techniques that should be used by players while performing these actions, are strictly defined.

While performing variatively beginning and finishing drills players have an opportunity to act offhand and apply technically different ways of performing techniques depending on a certain situation.

Training of the «technique of impulsive actions performance» should be paid special attention to, because players may have the advanced «technique of deliberate actions performance», yet may not cope with a task when it is necessary to choose one decision of many possible and implement the chosen one.

The low level of the efficiency of players' actions in such situations is usually associated with an underdeveloped so-called game thinking. Indeed, even possessing a fine game thinking, players may not be able to perform actions they have figured out in advance with a necessary quality, in case their level of the «technique of impulsive actions performance» is insufficient.

The main purpose of drills for perfection of the «game episodes technique», beginning from coming over the ball in open play, is the training of the technique of actions with the ball considering the specificity in performance of techniques according to the point of the pitch, and not tactical group and team interactions.

Coincidently, players' tactical interactions which are observed while performing drills with the ball by several players are bound to impact on the specificity of the techniques' performance.

Therefore certain drills may provide the performance of attacking actions by several players from the moment of coming over the ball till shooting on goal (attack in a whole) with elements of tactical interactions, while others may be reduced to their lowest terms for players to have an ability to improve certain specific elements of the «game episode technique».

The nature of the beginning of player's actions with the ball impacts the techniques performance. The structure of player's movements while performing initial actions with the ball essentially differs depending on whether he came over the ball after a tackle or interception, after a partner's pass or identified the moment of own actions beginning randomly, having already been in possession for a long time.

In this regard it is preferable for players training attacking actions not to possess the ball before beginning of a task performance, even while performing normally beginning drills, **but to begin their actions exactly from receiving the ball in one or another area of the pitch.**

For this purpose one of players (a defending player or a partner of an attacking player) or a coach may put the ball into a drill by means of:

– passes with a various degree of uncertainty in their performance and subsequently with a various degree of difficulty in receiving the ball by a player who has to begin attacking actions;
– imitation of actions of a player who tries to outplay an opponent in one or another area of the pitch and «suddenly loses» the ball after an active tackle.

It is possible to ensure that players come over the ball in a certain area of the pitch in gaming drills by means of the special construction of drills.

It is necessary to pay special attention to the quality aspect of the drills performance, namely: **to the quickness of players' taking proper decision in the beginning of attacking actions and speed and precision of the techniques performance.**

Depending on which area of the pitch attacking actions begin in, the priority may be placed on the quickness and precision of the attack beginning in certain cases, and on the quickness and precision of its undergoing in other.

It has to be noted that players may achieve the improvement of technical skills only by performing a large amount of repeats of actions with the ball.

Therefore a small number of outfield players should be involved in drills for perfection of the «game episodes technique», beginning from coming over the ball in open play, particularly no more than 3-4 players in each team in gaming drills.

CHAPTER 3. PERFECTION OF THE «GAME EPISODES TECHNIQUE» IN THE 18-YARD BOX

Characteristics of the drills construction

One of soccer regularities, being observed consistently in recent decades, is the ration of number of goals, scored from the 18-yard box and from beyond. Regardless of the competition level the great bulk of goals (more than 80%) is scored exactly from the 18-yard box.

Coincidently, the efficiency of shooting on goal, albeit higher than the efficiency of shooting from beyond, yet still is relatively small. The analysis of World Cup and European Championship matches shows that the ball hits the target approximately in 40 per cent of cases after shots, performed in the 18-yard box.

Taking into account that nearly one third of shots hitting the target is blocked by goalkeepers, it may be concluded there are large reserves for increasing the efficiency of shots performed in the 18-yard box:
– firstly, by means of increasing the precision of sending the ball on target;
– secondly, by means of perfection of abilities to outplay the goalkeeper in the context of sending the ball into the uncovered area of the goal.

Only certain players manage to shoot on goal from the 18-yard box a few times in competitive matches (it happens that even a striker doesn't get any opportunity to shoot on goal from the close range), that is clearly not enough for improvement in the «goalscoring skill». Therefore the only resource for increasing the efficiency of shots on goal and other actions in the 18-yard box are special drills.

It is necessary to consider at least two provision while constructing drills for training the goalscoring from the 18-yard box:
– the specificity of technique of shooting on goal from this area of the pitch;
– the possibility of a certain player performing a large amount of shots on goal in specialized conditions in the context of playing inside the 18-yard box.

The key factors, defining the specificity of performing shots on goal in the 18-yard box, are the time limit, causing attacking players to shoot as quick as possible, and the necessity to shoot with a physical contact with an opponent and from uncomfortable positions in many cases.

The analysis of games of top-teams allowed to find out certain specific characteristics of players performing shots on goal in the 18-yard box, presented in fig. 3.

Coincidently, researches of the transition of fitness in the precision of shooting on goal have revealed the following:
– if players have been training shots on goal with a certain power, while it is necessary to perform shots on goal from the same distance with another power, there is no fitness transition;
– if players have been training shots on goal with one direction of movement relative to the goal before shooting and body position relative to the direction of sending the ball at the moment of shooting, while it is required to shot on goal from the same distance in another direction of movements relative to the goal before shooting and body position relative to the direction of sending the ball at the moment of shooting, there is no fitness transition;
– if players have been training shots on goal with one position of the ball at the moment of shooting relative to the pitch surface (positioned on the pitch surface or at some height above the pitch surface), while it is required to perform shots on goal from the same distance with another position of the ball at the moment of shooting relative to the pitch surface, there is no fitness transition;

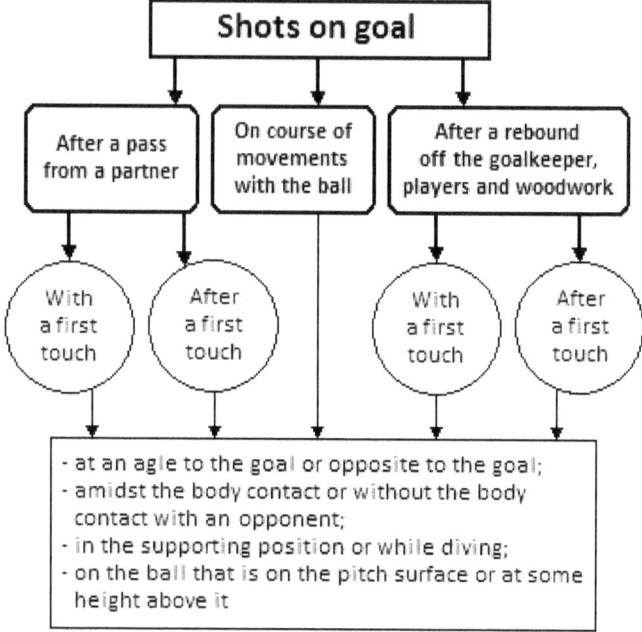

Fig. 3. Characteristics of performing shots on goal in the 18-yard box in open play, which should be considered while constructing drills for perfection of the «technique of game episodes» in the 18-yard box

– if players have been training shots on goal in easier condition in the context of requirements for oculogyric reactions (when there is an opportunity to trace the ball movement for sufficiently long time prior to shooting, when the ball approaches a players with a linear trajectory after coming in his sight), while it is necessary to perform shots on goal in more difficult conditions in the context of requirements for oculogyric reactions (when there is little time for tracing the ball movement before shooting, when the ball approaches to a player after coming in his sight while changing its trajectory as a result of bouncing off an obstacle), there is no fitness transition.

Therefore there is no fitness transition in the precision of shots on goal if players have to perform them in conditions when characteristics of movements performed with the ball (kinematics, dynamics, coordination of muscle work) change (relative to conditions of previous trainings).

Due to the fact that conditions of game in the 18-yard box differ markedly from conditions in which players act outside of it, even multiple repetition of shots on goal from the outside of the 18-yard box in training gives skilled players virtually nothing for increasing the efficiency of shots on goal performed in the 18-yard box.

It is necessary for players to train the goalscoring in the 18-yard box exactly to increase their prowess in attacking actions inside the box.

While constructing drills for perfection of the «technique of game episodes» inside the 18-yard box, one should look to the most typical game situations with a performance of certain techniques, both in the context of a point and way of shots of goal, resulting in goalscoring, and in the context of a point and nature of actions inside the box and beyond it, which precede the goalscoring (assists and movements with the ball, resulting in goalscoring).

Most of goals scored with a foot in open play from the 18-yard box are scored from the oval-shaped area which is positioned 2 meters and more from the goal-line to the 18-yard box line, around 25 meters across the width of the pitch and slightly displaced to the right relative to the goal (fig. 4).

80 to 90% of headers are scored from the area approx. 10x10 meters, positioned opposite to the goal 2 to 12 meters from the goal-line (fig. 5).

Passes resulting in goalscoring shots with a foot inside the 18-yard box are performed from two areas (to the right and to the left of the goal), each positioned between the sideline of the 18-yard box and the sideline of the goal area, lengthened to the 18-yard box line.

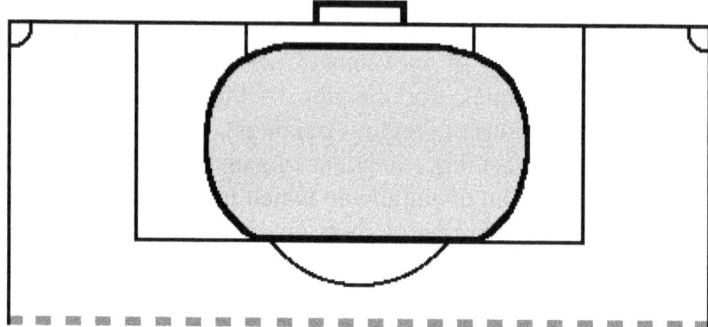

Fig. 4. Area from which the most of goals are scored with a foot in open play in the 18-yard box

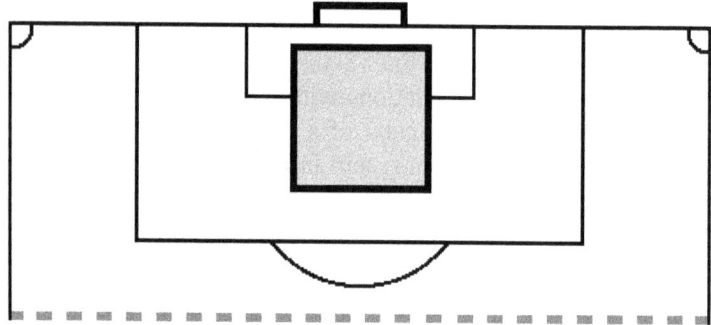

Fig. 5. Area in the 18-yard box from which the most of headers are scored

Overwhelmingly the ball is sent on a short and medium distance in parallel to the goal-line or in direction away from the goal both with or without crossing the central lengthwise axis of the pitch (fig. 6).

Passes resulting in goals scored with a head are mostly performed from areas, positioned to the left and to the right between the pitch sidelines and the 18-yard box sidelines lengthened into the pitch, and also from small areas in the 18-yard box, bordering with the box sidelines (fig. 7).

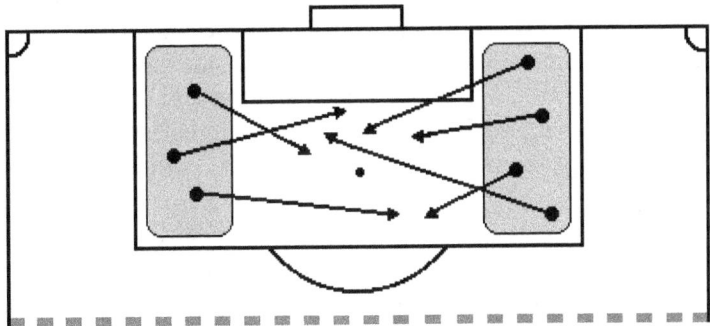

Fig. 6. Areas in the 18-yard box from which passes for shooting on goal with a foot should be performed, and directions of passes in drills for perfection the «game episodes technique» in the 18-yard box

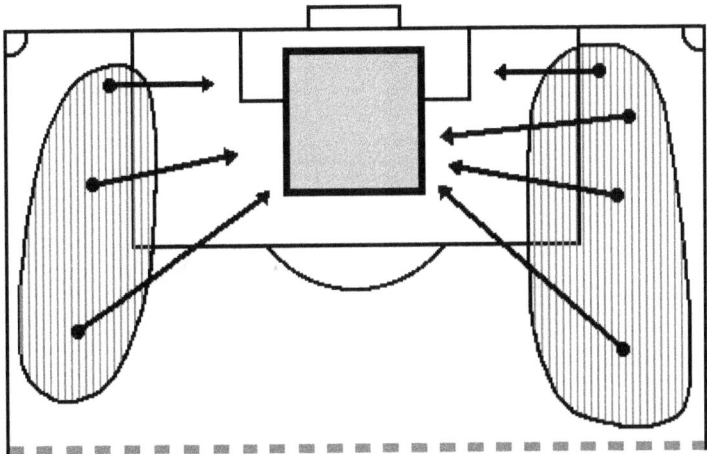

Fig. 7. Areas from which passes for shooting on goal with a head should be performed, and directions of passes in drills for perfection of the head-playing technique in the 18-yard box

Movements with the ball in the 18-yard box finishing with a goalscoring are performed by players in competitive matches at relatively short distances in following directions (fig. 8):

– perpendicularly or at some angle to the goal-line between sidelines of the 18-yard box and sidelines of the goal area lengthened into the pitch into areas nearly between angles of the goal area and 18-yard box (shots on goal are performed with sending the ball at some angle to the direction of movement);

– in parallel or at some angle to the goal-line away from the goal into areas nearly between angles of the goal area and 18-yard box (shots on goal are performed with sending the ball at a large angle to the direction of movement);

– perpendicularly or at some angle to the goal-line in corridor approx. 15 meters wide opposite to the goal area between the 18-yard box line and the penalty spot (shots on goal are performed with sending the ball into the direction coincident with the direction of dribbling or at some angle to the direction of movement).

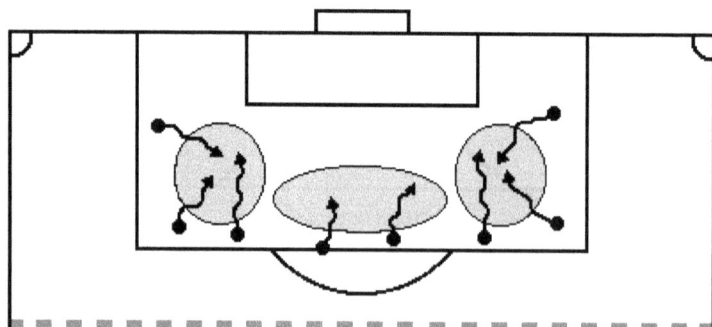

Fig. 8. Areas in the 18-yard box from which passes for shooting on goal with a foot should be performed, and directions of movements with the ball in drills for perfection the «game episodes technique» in the 18-yard box

Training the game technique while finishing the attacking actions with a foot kick

There are three kind of drills developed for perfection of the «game episodes technique» in the 18-yard box, beginning from coming over the ball that is already in open play, when an attack is being finished with a shot on goal by a foot:
- with a regular beginning and regular finishing of players' of actions with the ball;
- with a regular beginning and variative finishing of players' of actions with the ball;
- with a variative beginning and variative finishing of players' of actions with the ball.

Drills with a regular beginning and regular finishing of players' of actions with the ball

The main objective for drills with a regular beginning and regular finishing of players' actions with the ball in the 18-yard box is the perfection of the players' structure of movements while performing techniques in specific conditions, typical for game episodes in this area of the pitch.

Points of a beginning and finishing of actions with the ball, ways of their beginning and finishing in the performance technique are strictly defined in these drills.

Following are examples of drills with a regular beginning and regular finishing of players' actions with the ball for perfection of the «game episodes technique» in the 18-yard box in case of performing of a finishing shot on goal with a foot.

Task 1	
Task description	Requirements for task performance quality
Players' initial position, sequence of their actions and directions of movement 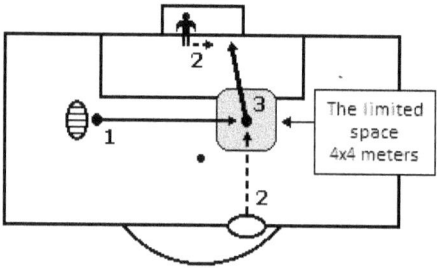 A partner of an attacking player sends the ball into the limited space across the pitch surface. An attacking players moves quickly into the limited space and shoots on goal with a first touch while diving obligingly. **Variants:** a) a partner of an attacking player sends the ball into the limited space with a bounce off the pitch surface and on air low-level; b) points of marking of the limited space and players' initial position are varied 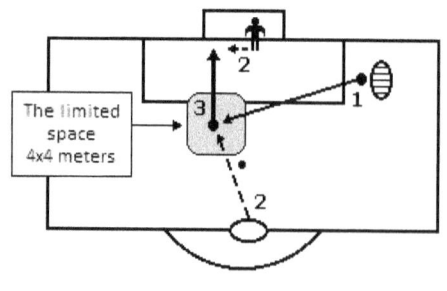	– a partner of an attacking player should send the ball into the limited space precisely and with the necessary speed; – an attacking player should begin to move into the limited space timely relative to the moment of the pass performing by a partner; – an attacking player should shoot on goal from the limited space exactly; – an attacking player should try to send the ball into the area of the goal, unprotected by the goalkeeper, every time

Soccer. Training the «game episodes technique», beginning from coming over the ball in open play

Task 2	
Task description	Requirements for task performance quality
Players' initial position, sequence of their actions and directions of movement 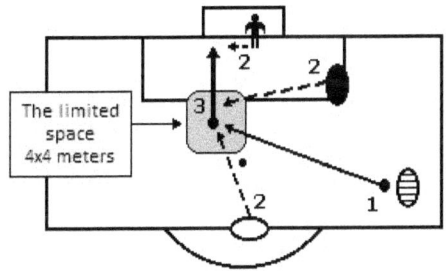 A partner of an attacking player sends the ball into the limited space across the pitch surface. An attacking players moves quickly into the limited space and shoots on goal with a first touch while diving obligingly. At the moment of a pass performing by an attacking player's partner a defending player begins to move into the limited space and tries to prevent an attacking player from shooting on goal, acting in the supporting position obligingly. A defending player is prohibited from intercepting the ball sent by a partner of an attacking player beyond the limited space. **Variants:** a) a partner of an attacking player sends the ball into the limited space with a bounce off the pitch surface; b) points of marking of the limited space and players' initial position are varied.	– a partner of an attacking player should send the ball into the limited space precisely and with the necessary speed; – an attacking player should begin to move into the limited space timely relative to the moment of the pass performing by a partner; – an attacking player should shoot on goal from the limited space exactly; – an attacking player should try to send the ball into the area of the goal, unprotected by the goalkeeper, every time

Task 2 continuation	
Task description	Requirements for task performance quality
[Diagram: Two field setups showing a 4x4 meter limited space with attacking players (1, 2) and a defending player (3), with arrows indicating passes and movement toward goal] **Note.** A distance at which a defending player is positioned in the initial position from the limited space should be such that he could come up with an attacking player when the latter shoots on goal, beginning the movement when a partner of an attacking player performs a pass, but at the same time that an attacking player could shoot on goal from the limited space with a first touch while diving, acting with a maximum speed	

Soccer. Training the «game episodes technique», beginning from coming over the ball in open play

Task 3	
Task description	Requirements for task performance quality
Players' initial position, sequence of their actions and directions of movement A defending player positions himself back to the goal. 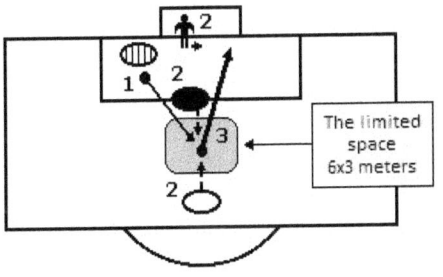 A partner of an attacking player sends the ball into the limited space across the pitch surface to the left or to the right from a defending player so that he couldn't see a moment of a pass performance. An attacking player quickly moves into the limited space and shoots on goal in any way (in supporting position or while diving) **with a first touch obligingly**. At the moment when an attacking player begins to move into the limited space a defending player begins to move into the limited space and tries to prevent an attacking player from shooting on goal, **acting in the limited space obligingly**. A defending player is prohibited from: – tracing the moment of performing a pass by a partner of an attacking player; – intercepting the ball sent by a partner of an attacking player beyond the limited space.	– a partner of an attacking player should send the ball into the limited space precisely and with the necessary speed; – an attacking player should begin to move into the limited space timely relative to the moment of the pass performing by a partner; – an attacking player should shoot on goal from the limited space exactly; – an attacking player should perform shots on goal from any, even inconvenient positions; – an attacking player should try to send the ball into the area of the goal, unprotected by the goalkeeper, every time

Task 3 continuation	
Task description	Requirements for task performance quality
Variants: a) a partner of an attacking player sends the ball into the limited space with a bounce off the pitch surface and on air low-level; b) points of marking of the limited space and players' initial position are varied. *[Diagram: The limited space 6x3 meters]* **Note.** A distance at which a defending player is positioned in the initial position from the limited space should be such that he could come up with an attacking player when the latter shoots on goal, beginning the movement when an attacking player begins to move into the limited space, but at the same time that an attacking player could shoot on goal from the limited space with a first touch while diving, acting with a maximum speed	

Task 4		
	Task description	Requirements for task performance quality
Players' initial position, sequence of their actions and directions of movement 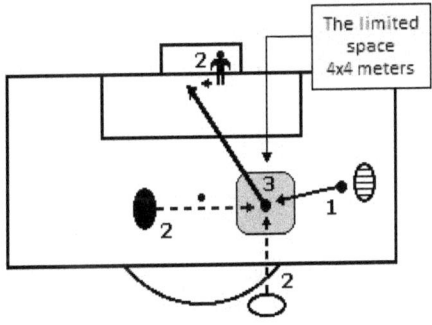 A partner of an attacking player sends the ball into the limited space across the pitch surface. An attacking players moves quickly into the limited space and shoots on goal **with a first touch in the supporting position obligingly.** At the moment of a pass performing by an attacking player's partner a defending player begins to move into the limited space and tries to prevent an attacking player from shooting on goal. **Variants:** a) a partner of an attacking player sends the ball into the limited space with a slight bounce off the pitch surface, while an attacking player shoots in goal **at the moment when the ball is at some height above the pitch surface obligingly;** b) points of marking of the limited space and players' initial position are varied.		– a partner of an attacking player should send the ball into the limited space precisely and with the necessary speed; – an attacking player should begin to move into the limited space timely relative to the moment of the pass performing by a partner; – an attacking player should shoot on goal from the limited space exactly; – an attacking player should try to send the ball into the area of the goal, unprotected by the goalkeeper, every time

Task 4 continuation	
Task description	Requirements for task performance quality
[diagram: limited space 4x4 meters with players positioned; attacking and defending movements shown]	
Note. A distance at which a defending player is positioned in the initial position from the limited space should be such that he could come up with an attacking player when the latter shoots on goal, beginning the movement when a partner of an attacking player performs a pass, but at the same time that an attacking player could shoot on goal from the limited space with a first touch in the supporting position, acting with a maximum speed	

Task 5	
Task description	Requirements for task performance quality
Players' initial position, sequence of their actions and directions of movement An attacking player positions himself back to the goal. 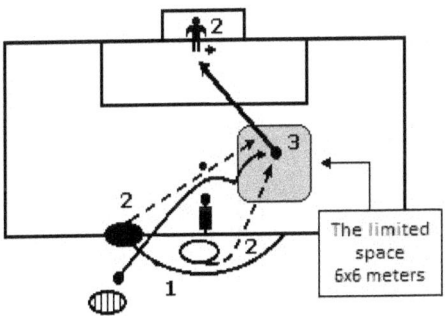 A partner of an attacking player sends the ball into the limited space above the mannequin, designating a defending player, with a bounce off the pitch surface. An attacking player quickly moves into the limited space and shoots on goal **with a first touch obligingly at the moment when the bounced ball is at some height above the pitch surface.** At the moment of a pass performing by an attacking player's partner a defending player begins to move into the limited space and tries to prevent an attacking player from shooting on goal. **Variants:** a) points of marking of the limited space and players' initial position are varied;	– a partner of an attacking player should send the ball into the limited space precisely and with the necessary speed; – an attacking player should begin to move into the limited space timely relative to the moment of the pass performing by a partner; – an attacking player should shoot on goal from the limited space exactly; – an attacking player should perform shots on goal from any, even inconvenient positions; – an attacking player should try to send the ball into the area of the goal, unprotected by the goalkeeper, every time

Task 5 continuation	
Task description	Requirements for task performance quality
b) an attacking player receives the bounced ball and shoots on goal from the limited space **with a second touch obligingly at the moment when the ball is at some height above the pitch surface;** c) an attacking player positions face to the goal in initial position and runs into the limited space, **moving in an arc.** 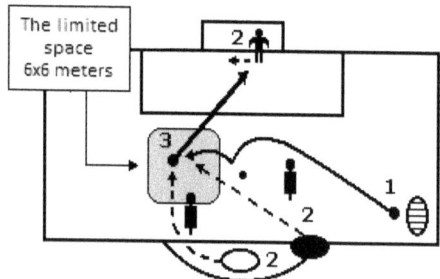 **Note.** A distance at which a defending player is positioned in the initial position from the limited space should be such that he could come up with an attacking player when the latter shoots on goal, beginning the movement when a partner of an attacking player performs a pass, but at the same time that an attacking player could shoot on goal from the limited space with a first or second touch, acting with a maximum speed	

Task 6	
Task description	Requirements for task performance quality
Players' initial position, sequence of their actions and directions of movement 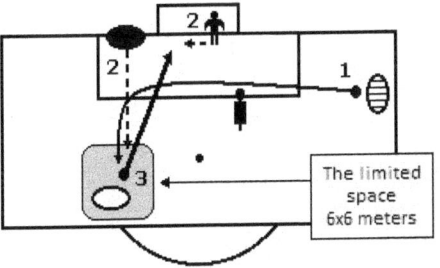 A partner of an attacking player sends the ball into the limited space above the mannequin, designating a defending player. An attacking player shoots on goal with a foot from the limited space **with a first touch without allowing the ball to touch the pitch surface obligingly (with a volley).** At the moment of a pass performing by an attacking player's partner a defending player begins to move into the limited space and tries to prevent an attacking player from shooting on goal. **Variants:** a) points of marking of the limited space and players' initial position are varied; b) an attacking player receives the ball and shoots on goal with a second touch without allowing the ball to touch the pitch surface not even once;	– a partner of an attacking player should send the ball into the limited space precisely and with the necessary speed; – in cases when he is positioned beyond the limited space in the initial position, an attacking player should begin moving into the limited space timely relative to the moment of a partner performing a pass; – an attacking player should shoot on goal from the limited space exactly; – an attacking player should perform shots on goal from any, even inconvenient positions, including while diving; – an attacking player should try to send the ball into the area of the goal, unprotected by the goalkeeper, every time

Task 6 continuation	
Task description	Requirements for task performance quality
c) in the initial position an attacking player is positioned at some distance from the limited space and moves into the limited space in different directions after a pass from a partner to shoot on goal. 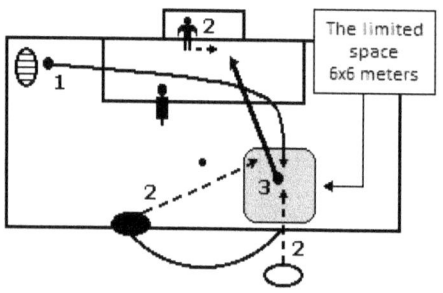 **Note.** A distance at which a defending player is positioned in the initial position from the limited space should be such that he could come up with an attacking player when the latter shoots on goal, beginning the movement when a partner of an attacking player performs a pass, but at the same time that an attacking player could shoot on goal from the limited space with a first or second touch, without allowing the ball to touch the pitch surface not even once	

Soccer. Training the «game episodes technique», beginning from coming over the ball in open play

Task 7	
Task description	Requirements for task performance quality
Players' initial position, sequence of their actions and directions of movement 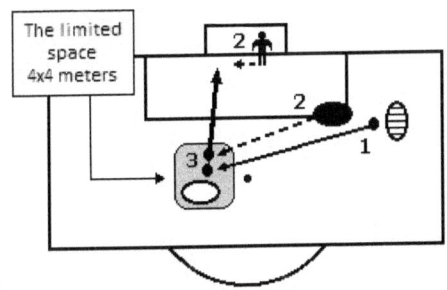 A partner of an attacking player sends the ball to an attacking player into the limited space across the pitch surface. An attacking player receives the ball and shoots on goal from the limited space **with a second touch obligingly**. At the moment of a pass performing by an attacking player's partner a defending player begins to move into the limited space and tries to prevent an attacking player from shooting on goal. A defending player is prohibited from intercepting the ball sent by a partner of an attacking player beyond the limited space. **Variants:** a) points of marking of the limited space and players' initial position are varied; b) a partner of an attacking player sends the ball into the limited space with a bounce off the pitch surface and on air low-level;	– a partner of an attacking player should send the ball into the limited space precisely and with the necessary speed; – in cases when an attacking player is positioned in the initial position beyond the limited space, a defending player should perform a pass to an attacking player timely relative to the moment when the latter begins to move into the limited space; – an attacking player should shoot on goal from the limited space exactly; – having received the ball, an attacking player should shoot on goal with a second touch without a delay and with a maximum speed; – an attacking player should try to send the ball into the area of the goal, unprotected by the goalkeeper, every time

Task 7 continuation	
Task description	Requirements for task performance quality
c) in the initial position an attacking player is positioned at some distance from the limited space and moves into the limited space in different directions after a pass from a partner to shoot on goal. 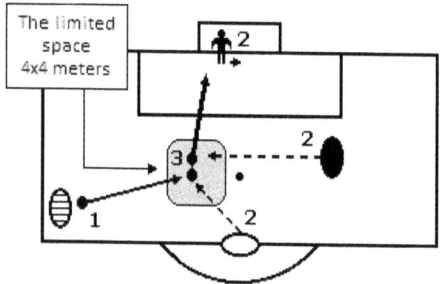 **Note.** A distance at which a defending player is positioned in the initial position from the limited space should be such that he could come up with an attacking player when the latter shoots on goal, beginning the movement when a partner of an attacking player performs a pass, but at the same time that an attacking player could shoot on goal from the limited space with a second touch, acting with a maximum speed and precision	

Task 8

Task description	Requirements for task performance quality
Players' initial position, sequence of their actions and directions of movement 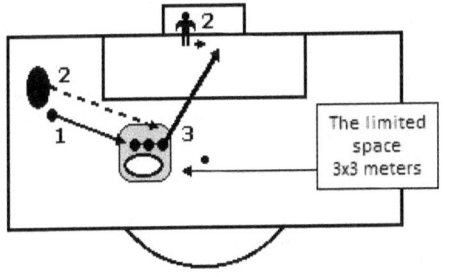 A defending player sends the ball to an attacking player into the limited space across the pitch surface. An attacking player receives the ball, prepares it for a shot with a second touch and shoots on goal from the limited space **with a third touch obligingly**. Having performed a pass, a defending player begins to move into the limited space and tries to prevent an attacking player from shooting on goal. **Variants:** a) a defending player sends the ball into the limited space with a bounce off the pitch surface and on air low-level; b) a defending player may pass the ball to an attacking player so that it is difficult for him to receive it by means of sending the ball with increased speed and on air low-level or with a bounce off the pitch surface;	– a defending player should send the ball into the limited space precisely; – in cases when an attacking player is positioned in the initial position beyond the limited space, a defending player should perform a pass to an attacking player timely relative to the moment when the latter begins to move into the limited space; – an attacking player should shoot on goal from the limited space exactly; – having received the ball, an attacking player should prepare it for the shot and shoot on goal with a third touch without a delay and with a maximum speed; – an attacking player should try to send the ball into the area of the goal, unprotected by the goalkeeper, every time

Task 8 continuation	
Task description	Requirements for task performance quality
c) points of marking of the limited space and players' initial position are varied; d) in the initial position an attacking player is positioned at some distance from the limited space and moves into the limited space in different directions after a pass from a defending player to shoot on goal. *[Diagram: The limited space 3x3 meters, with players numbered 1, 2, 3, 4]* **Note.** A distance at which a defending player is positioned in the initial position from the limited space should be such that he could come up with an attacking player when the latter shoots on goal, beginning the movement after performing a pass, but at the same time that an attacking player could shoot on goal from the limited space with a second touch, acting with a maximum speed and precision	

Task 9

Task description	Requirements for task performance quality
Players' initial position, sequence of their actions and directions of movement 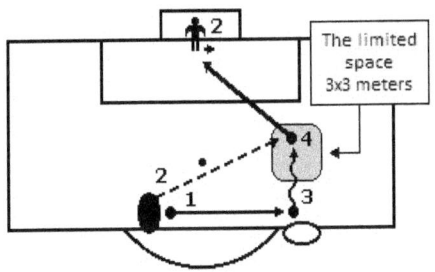 A defending player sends the ball to an attacking player, positioned on the 18-yard box line, across the pitch surface. An attacking player receives the ball, quickly moves into the limited space with it and shoots on goal. Having performed a pass, a defending player begins to move into the limited space and tries to prevent an attacking player from shooting on goal. **Variants:** a) a defending player sends the ball to an attacking player with a bounce off the pitch surface and on air low-level; b) a defending player may pass the ball to an attacking player so that it is difficult for him to receive it by means of sending the ball with increased speed and on air low-level or with a bounce off the pitch surface; c) points of marking of the limited space and players' initial position are varied;	– a defending player should send the ball to an attacking player precisely at foot; – in cases when an attacking player is positioned in the initial position beyond the 18-yard box, a defending player should perform a pass to an attacking player towards the 18-yard box line timely relative to the moment when the latter begins to move into the 18-yard box; – an attacking player should quickly move into the limited space with the ball and shoot on goal; – an attacking player should shoot on goal also with a physical contact with a defending player; – an attacking player should shoot on goal from the limited space exactly;

Task 9 continuation	
Task description	Requirements for task performance quality
d) an attacking player positions in the initial position at some distance from the 18-yard box line beyond it and moves towards this line in different directions for receiving the ball from a defending player and then moves with the ball into the limited space for shooting on goal.	– an attacking player should try to send the ball into the area of the goal, unprotected by the goalkeeper, every time
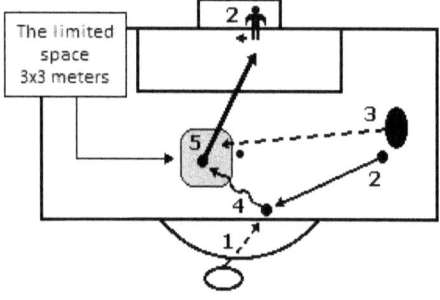	
Note. A distance at which a defending player is positioned in the initial position from the limited space should be such that he could come up with an attacking player when the latter shoots on goal, beginning the movement after performing a pass, but at the same time that an attacking player could shoot on goal from the limited space, acting with a maximum speed and precision	

Drills with a regular beginning and variative finishing of players' of actions with the ball

The main objective for drills with a regular beginning and variative finishing of players' actions with the ball is the training of techniques' performance in the 18-yard box in situations, when taking decision on continuation of actions with the ball happens depending on nature of the opponent's countering and partners' assistance.

In these drills finishing actions may be performed either individually or with participation of two or three players.

Following are examples of drills with a regular beginning and variative finishing of players' actions with the ball for perfection of the «game episodes technique» in the 18-yard box in case of performing of shots on goal with a foot.

Task 1	
Task description	Requirements for task performance quality
Players' initial position, sequence of their actions and directions of movement 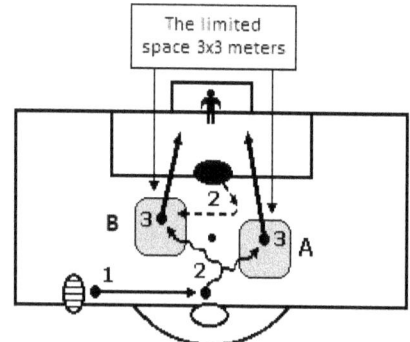 A partner of an attacking player sends the ball to an attacking player, positioned on the 18-yard box line, across the pitch surface. An attacking player receives the ball, quickly moves with it into the closer (variant A) or distant (variant B) limited space and shoots on goal. When an attacking player makes his first touch of the ball, a defending player begins to move towards an attacking player and tries to prevent him from shooting on goal. **Variants:** a) a partner of an attacking player sends the ball to an attacking player with a bounce off the pitch surface and on air low-level; b) points of marking of limited spaces and players' initial position are varied;	– a partner of an attacking player should send the ball to an attacking player precisely at foot; – in cases when an attacking player is positioned in the initial position beyond the 18-yard box, his partner should perform a pass to an attacking player towards the 18-yard box line timely relative to the moment when the latter begins to move into the 18-yard box; – an attacking player should quickly move into the closer or distant limited space with the ball and shoot on goal; – an attacking player should shoot on goal from the limited space exactly (closer or distant from him); – an attacking player should try to send the ball into the area of the goal, unprotected by the goalkeeper, every time

Soccer. Training the «game episodes technique», beginning from coming over the ball in open play

Task 1 continuation	
Task description	Requirements for task performance quality
c) an attacking player positions in the initial position at some distance from the 18-yard box line beyond it and moves towards this line in different directions for receiving the ball from a partner and then moves with the ball into the closer or distant limited space for shooting on goal. The limited space 3x3 meters **Note.** A distance at which a defending player is positioned in the initial position from the closer limited space should be such that he could come up with an attacking player when the latter makes a first touch, beginning the movement after performing a pass, but at the same time that an attacking player could shoot on goal from the closer or distant limited space, acting with a maximum speed and precision	

Task 2

Task description	Requirements for task performance quality
Players' initial position, sequence of their actions and directions of movement 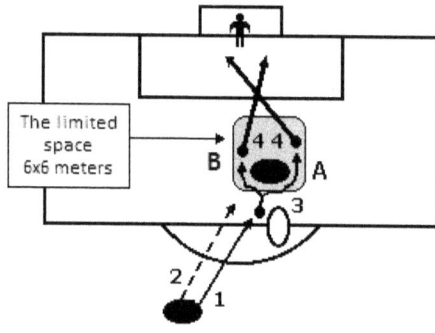 A defending player, positioned beyond the 18-yard box, sends the ball to an attacking player, positioned on the 18-yard box line, across the pitch surface. An attacking player receives the ball, quickly moves with it into the limited space, beats a defending player, positioned in the limited space, to the left (variant B) or to the right (variant A) and shoots on goal. Having performed a pass, a defending player, positioned beyond the 18-yard box, begins to move into the limited space and tries to prevent an attacking player from shooting on goal. **Variants:** a) a defending player sends the ball to an attacking player with a bounce off the pitch surface and on air low-level; b) points of marking of limited spaces and players' initial position are varied;	– a defending player should send the ball to an attacking player precisely at foot; – in cases when an attacking player is positioned in the initial position beyond the 18-yard box, a defending player should perform a pass to an attacking player towards the 18-yard box line timely relative to the moment when the latter begins to move into the 18-yard box; – an attacking player should quickly move into the limited space with the ball, beat a defending player and shoot on goal; – an attacking player should shoot on goal from the limited space exactly; – an attacking player should try to send the ball into the area of the goal, unprotected by the goalkeeper, every time

Soccer. Training the «game episodes technique», beginning from coming over the ball in open play

Task 2 continuation	
Task description	Requirements for task performance quality
c) an attacking player positions in the initial position at some distance from the 18-yard box line beyond it and moves towards this line in different directions for receiving the ball from a defending player and then moves with the ball into the limited space for shooting on goal. *[Diagram showing the limited space 6x6 meters with players B, A, and positions 1, 2, 3, 4, 5]* **Note.** A distance at which a defending player is positioned in the initial position beyond the 18-yard box from the limited space should be such that he could come up with an attacking player when the latter shoots on goal, beginning the movement after performing a pass, but at the same time that an attacking player could shoot on goal from the limited space, acting with a maximum speed and precision	

Task 3

Task description	Requirements for task performance quality
Players' initial position, sequence of their actions and directions of movement 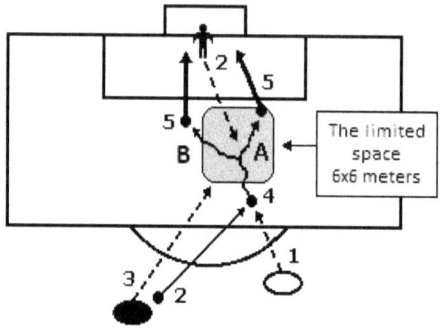 A defending player sends the ball into the 18-yard box to an attacking player, moving from beyond the 18-yard box in it, across the pitch surface. An attacking player receives the ball and quickly moves into the limited space with it. After a pass to an attacking player from a defending player the goalkeeper moves from the goal into the limited space. An attacking player beats the goalkeeper inside the limited space to the left (variant B) or to the right (variant A) side and shoots on goal from any point of the 18-yard box. Having performed a pass, a defending player begins to move into the limited space and tries to prevent an attacking player from beating the goalkeeper and shooting on goal.	– a defending player should perform a pass to an attacking player towards the 18-yard box line timely relative to the moment when the latter begins to move into the 18-yard box; – a defending player should send the ball to an attacking player so that he could receive it, moving with a high speed; – an attacking player should act with a maximum precision when receives the ball; – an attacking player should quickly move into the limited space with the ball and beat the goalkeeper; – the goalkeeper should move from the goal into the limited space for catching or blocking the ball timely; – an attacking player should beat the goalkeeper in the limited space exactly

Soccer. Training the «game episodes technique», beginning from coming over the ball in open play

Task 3 continuation	
Task description	Requirements for task performance quality
Variants: a) a defending player sends the ball to an attacking player with a bounce off the pitch surface and on air low-level; b) points of marking of limited spaces and players' initial position are varied; c) an attacking player is permitted to shoot on goal from the limited space without previously beating the goalkeeper. **Note.** A distance at which a defending player is positioned in the initial position beyond the 18-yard box from the limited space should be such that he could come up with an attacking player when the latter beats the goalkeeper and shoots on goal, beginning the movement after performing a pass, but at the same time that an attacking player could beat the goalkeeper in the limited space and shoot on goal, acting with a maximum speed and precision	

Task 4	
Task description	Requirements for task performance quality
Players' initial position, sequence of their actions and directions of movement 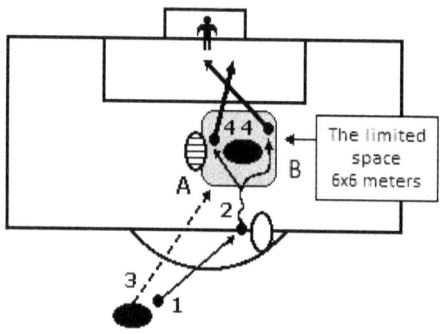 A defending player, positioned beyond the 18-yard box, sends the ball to an attacking player, positioned on the 18-yard box line, across the pitch surface. An attacking player receives the ball, begins to move with it quickly towards the limited space and sends the ball to a partner into the limited space for shooting on goal **from it with a first or second touch** (variant A) or beats a defending player in the limited space and shoots on goal **from the limited space** (variant B). Having performed a pass, a defending player, positioned beyond the 18-yard box, begins to move into the limited space and tries to prevent attacking players from shooting on goal.	– a defending player should send the ball to an attacking player precisely at foot; – in cases when an attacking player is positioned in the initial position beyond the 18-yard box, a defending player should perform a pass to an attacking player towards the 18-yard box line timely relative to the moment when the latter begins to move into the 18-yard box; – an attacking player should quickly move with the ball towards the limited space, make a pass to a partner for shooting on goal from the limited space or beat a defending player and shoot on goal; – a partner of an attacking player should shoot on goal with a first or second touch obligingly;

Task 4 continuation	
Task description	Requirements for task performance quality
Variants: a) a defending player sends the ball to an attacking player with a bounce off the pitch surface and on air low-level; b) points of marking of limited spaces and players' initial position are varied; c) in initial position an attacking player is positioned at some distance from the 18-yard box beyond it and moves into it in different directions to receive the ball.	– attacking players should shoot on goal from the limited space exactly; – attacking players should try to send the ball into the area of the goal, unprotected by the goalkeeper, every time
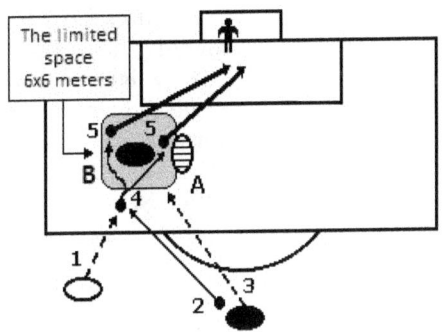	
Note. A distance at which a defending player is positioned in the initial position beyond the 18-yard box from the limited space should be such that he could come up with attacking players when the latter shoots on goal, beginning the movement after performing a pass, but at the same time that attacking players could shoot on goal from the limited space, acting with a maximum speed and precision	

Task 5	
Task description	Requirements for task performance quality
Players' initial position, sequence of their actions and directions of movement 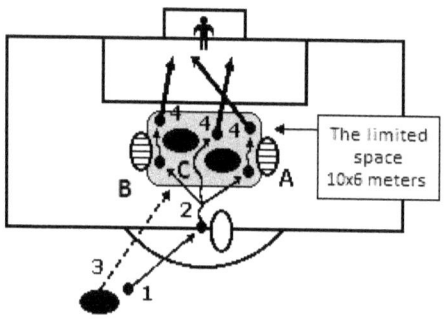 A defending player, positioned beyond the 18-yard box, sends the ball to an attacking player, positioned on the 18-yard box line, across the pitch surface. An attacking player receives the ball, begins to move with it quickly towards the limited space and sends the ball to one of partners into the limited space for shooting on goal **from it with a first or second touch** (variant A and B) or beats defending players in the limited space and shoots on goal **from the limited space** (variant C). Having performed a pass, a defending player, positioned beyond the 18-yard box, begins to move into the limited space and tries to prevent attacking players from shooting on goal.	– a defending player should send the ball to an attacking player precisely at foot; – in cases when an attacking player is positioned in the initial position beyond the 18-yard box, a defending player should perform a pass to an attacking player towards the 18-yard box line timely relative to the moment when the latter begins to move into the 18-yard box; – an attacking player should quickly move with the ball towards the limited space, make a pass to one of partner for shooting on goal from the limited space or beat a defending player and shoot on goal; – partners of an attacking player should shoot on goal with a first or second touch obligingly;

Soccer. Training the «game episodes technique», beginning from coming over the ball in open play

Task 5 continuation	
Task description	Requirements for task performance quality
Variants: a) a defending player sends the ball to an attacking player with a bounce off the pitch surface and on air low-level; b) points of marking of limited spaces and players' initial position are varied; c) in initial position an attacking player is positioned at some distance from the 18-yard box beyond it and moves into it in different directions to receive the ball.	– attacking players should shoot on goal from the limited space exactly; – attacking players should try to send the ball into the area of the goal, unprotected by the goalkeeper, every time
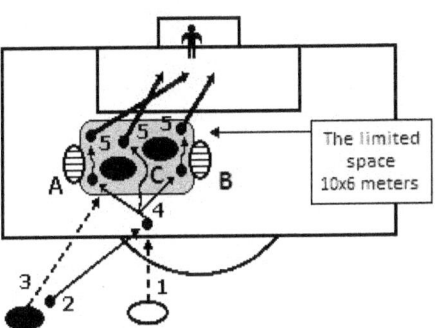	
Note. A distance at which a defending player is positioned in the initial position beyond the 18-yard box from the limited space should be such that he could come up with attacking players when the latter shoots on goal, beginning the movement after performing a pass, but at the same time that attacking players could shoot on goal from the limited space, acting with a maximum speed and precision	

Task 6	
Task description	Requirements for task performance quality
Players' initial position, sequence of their actions and directions of movement 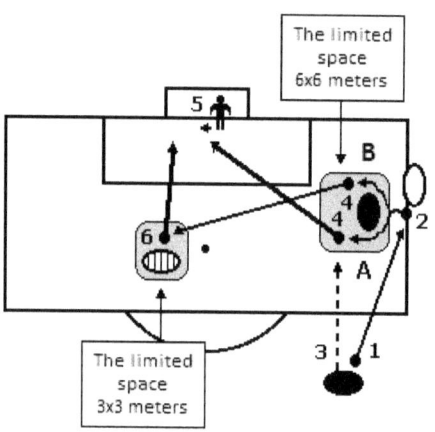 A defending player, positioned beyond the 18-yard box, sends the ball to an attacking player, positioned on the 18-yard box sideline, across the pitch surface. An attacking player receives the ball, quickly moves with it into the limited space at the 18-yard box sideline, beat a defending player, positioned in this space, to the left side and shoots on goal from the limited space (variant A) or to the right side and performs a pass to a partner into the limited space opposite to the goal for shooting on goal **with a first touch** (variant B).	– a defending player should send the ball to an attacking player precisely at foot; – in cases when an attacking player is positioned in the initial position beyond the 18-yard box, a defending player should perform a pass to an attacking player towards the 18-yard box sideline timely relative to the moment when the latter begins to move into the 18-yard box; – an attacking player should quickly move with the ball into the limited space, make a pass to a partner for shooting on goal from the limited space opposite to the goal or beat a defending player and shoot on goal; – a partner of an attacking player should shoot on goal with a first touch obligingly;

Task 6 continuation	
Task description	Requirements for task performance quality
Having performed a pass, a defending player, positioned beyond the 18-yard box, begins to move into the limited space at the 18-yard box sideline and tries to prevent an attacking player from passing to a partner in the limited space opposite to the goal or shooting on goal. **Variants:** a) a defending player sends the ball to an attacking player with a bounce off the pitch surface and on air low-level; b) points of marking of limited spaces and players' initial position are varied; c) in initial position an attacking player is positioned at some distance from the 18-yard box sideline beyond the box and moves towards the sideline in different directions to receive the ball. **Note.** A distance at which a defending player is positioned in the initial position beyond the 18-yard box from the limited space at the 18-yard box sideline should be such that he could come up with an attacking player when the latter shoots on goal or performing a pass to a partner, beginning the movement after performing a pass, but at the same time that an attacking player could shoot on goal or perform a pass to a partner from the limited space, acting with a maximum speed and precision	– attacking players should shoot on goal from limited spaces exactly; – attacking players should try to send the ball into the area of the goal, unprotected by the goalkeeper, every time

Task 7	
Task description	Requirements for task performance quality
Players' initial position, sequence of their actions and directions of movement An attacking player is positioned back to the opponents' goal in the limited space opposite to the goal area corner. 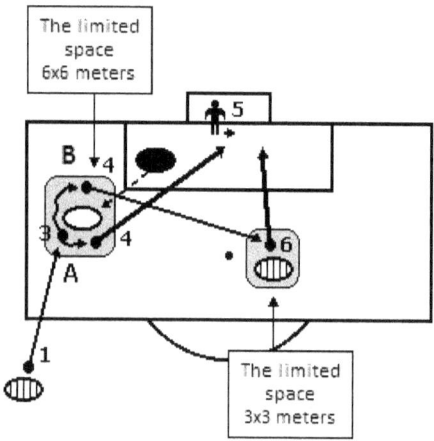 A partner of an attacking player, positioned beyond the 18-yard box, sends the ball to an attacking player into the limited space across the pitch surface. An attacking player receives the ball back to the goal, beats a defending player, positioned in the limited space, to the left side and shoots on goal variant A) or to the right side and performs a pass to a partner into the limited space opposite to the goal for shooting on goal **with a first touch** (variant B).	– a partner of an attacking player should send the ball to an attacking player precisely at foot; – in cases when an attacking player is positioned in the initial position at some distance from the limited space, positioned at the goal area corner, a partner of an attacking player should perform a pass to him timely relative to the moment when the latter begins to move into this limited space; – an attacking player should shoot on goal also with a physical contact with an opponent; – an attacking player should quickly beat a defending player and perform a pass to a partner or a shot on goal; – a partner of an attacking player should shoot on goal with a first touch obligingly;

Task 7 continuation	
Task description	Requirements for task performance quality
At the moment when a partner of an attacking player performs a pass, a defending player begins to move into the limited space opposite to the goal area corner and tries to prevent an attacking player from passing to a partner in the limited space opposite to the goal or shooting on goal. **Variants:** a) a partner of an attacking player sends the ball to an attacking player with a bounce off the pitch surface and on air low-level; b) points of marking of limited spaces and players' initial position are varied; c) initial position an attacking player is positioned at some distance from the limited space, positioned at the goal area corner, and moves into this space in different directions for receiving the ball while being back to the opponents' goal. **Note.** A distance at which a defending player is positioned in the initial position from the limited space at the goal area corner should be such that he could come up with an attacking player when the latter receives the ball, beginning the movement when a partner of an attacking player performs a pass, but at the same time that an attacking player could receive the ball in the limited space back to the goal, acting with a maximum speed and precision	– attacking players should shoot on goal from limited spaces exactly; – attacking players should try to send the ball into the area of the goal, unprotected by the goalkeeper, every time

Task 8

Task description	Requirements for task performance quality
Players' initial position, sequence of their actions and directions of movement 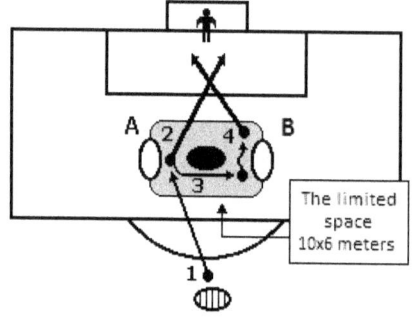 A partner of attacking players sends the ball to one of them into the limited space across the pitch surface. An attacking player shoots on goal (variant A) or performs a pass to another attacking player for shooting on goal from the limited space (variant B), with a first touch or after handling the ball. A defending player tries to prevent attacking players from shooting on goal. A defending player is prohibited from intercepting the ball sent by a partner of attacking players beyond the limited space. Number of passes to attacking players – no more than one. Number of touches of the ball by each of attacking players – no more than three.	– a partner of attacking players should send the ball to them precisely at foot; – attacking players should act with a maximum precision when receives the ball; – attacking players should quickly perform a shot on goal or a pass to a partner for shooting on goal; – attacking players should shoot on goal from the limited space exactly; – attacking players should shoot on goal also with a physical contact with an opponent; – attacking players should try to send the ball into the area of the goal, unprotected by the goalkeeper, every time

Soccer. Training the «game episodes technique», beginning from coming over the ball in open play

Task 8 continuation	
Task description	Requirements for task performance quality
Variants: a) a partner of attacking players sends the ball to them with a bounce off the pitch surface and on air low-level; b) points of marking of limited spaces and players' initial position are varied	

Drills with a variative beginning and variative finishing of players' of actions with the ball

With reference to the specificity of soccer there are virtually no ideal drills, performing which player could act in totally game conditions and perform a large amount of techniques repeats coincidently.

Therefore while organizing drills for the perfection of the «game episodes technique» it is necessary to look for a compromise, resulting in that players are able to perform such necessary values of repeats of actions with the ball that make the improvement of technical skills possible, without sacrificing the utterly possible specialization of conditions of the drills performance.

Gaming drills mostly response to conditions which have to be observed to achieve the improvement in prowess of attacking actions in the 18-yard box, among drills with a variative beginning and finishing.

Firstly it refers to various variants of **«playing soccer with the contiguous goals»,** protected by goalkeepers, with certain restrictions and objectives and a small number of players in teams. It has to be noted that, while performing these drills, the goal of a standard size is obligingly used, and all the players (either goalkeepers and outfield players) must act with a full responsibility and highest commitment, as in competitive matches.

The worth of gaming drills with the contiguous goals is that it's possible not only to achieve the performance of a large amount of shots on goal in most specialized conditions, but also to regulate the working load precisely enough by means of:

– varying of the playing ground size;
– change in number of outfield players in teams;
– imposition of various limitations for possession by certain players of a team as a whole (over time, number of touches of the ball, number of passes in attack).

Moreover, during these drills outfield players can improve not only attacking actions in the 18-yard box, but also defensive ones, which also differ from defensive actions, performed outside the 18-yard box, in their turn.

While participating in gaming drills with the contiguous goals, goalkeepers get an opportunity to train plenty of time exactly in conditions, in which the most part of goals is scored in soccer, and develop the most important for them reactions of anticipation of the shooting moment and direction of the ball by actions of player, performing a shot on goal, and anticipation of the development of play situations.

At the same time in gaming drills with the contiguous goals (without a special organization with additional tasks) there are no shots on goal with a foot after a pass at the long distance, and also there is relatively low probability that players would shoot on goal with a head.

Applying certain methodological techniques of organization of gaming drills with the contiguous goals allows to:

– intentionally improve the technique of performance of certain techniques while performing attacking and defensive actions in the 18-yard box;

– regulate the working load precisely enough with an aim to improve players' functional capabilities;

– train a wide range of individual and group tactical actions (attacking and defensive) either on the spot or strictly on a task.

The following methodological techniques may be applied.

1. Change in size and shape of the playing ground and of position of the goal mounting.

Change of size of the playing ground allows to provide the congestion of players in certain areas and thus emulate goalscoring episodes in competitive matches in the context of the space deficit.

Change of size of the playing ground may encourage players to use one or another way of delivery of the ball to the shooting position to a greater extent. Specifically, players get more opportunities to perform lateral (flank) passes on the short and wide playing ground (fig. 9A), and to move with the ball, overcoming sufficiently large space on the narrow and long one (fig. 9B).

Mounting of the goal so that they are not opposite, but somewhat dislocated relative to each other every which way along the goal-line (fig. 9c), allows to increase the number of shots on goal, performed by players at an angle to the goal.

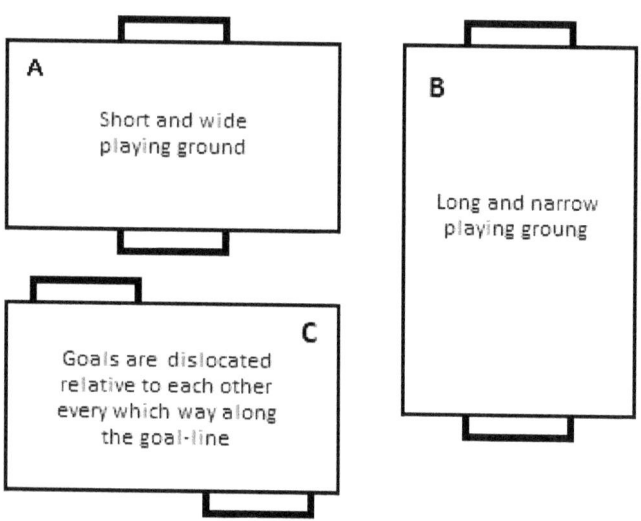

Fig. 9. Examples of the playing ground shape and the goal mounting while constructing gaming drills with the contiguous goals

2. Varying the number of players, participating in a drill.

Generally the number of outfield players, participating in gaming drills with the contiguous goals, may vary from one to ten, although it has to be considered that it is impossible to achieve a large volume of repeats of actions with the ball by each player with a high number of players in each team.

The optimal number of participants while training the technique of play in the 18-yard box is one to four outfield players in each team. Also, «neutral» players may be introduced into these drills (either one or two), who play constantly for those possessing the ball and may ease the training of some attacking actions for other players.

With the object of players performing attacking actions during drills with the contiguous goals in real game conditions, where defending players generally have an advantage in numbers over attackers in the 18-yard box, the following methodological technique may be employed: the number of players in one team is increased by one with upon condition that these players come short of skill relative to players from a team playing with the numerical disadvantage. For instance, four teenage defending players may stand up against three attacking players of top-class.

By changing the number of participants in drill and size of the playing ground simultaneously, it is possible to adjust the congestion of players in certain space, the frequency of players' contacts with the ball, the working load coming to players, and also to train various tactical interactions.

3. Encouraging players to perform certain actions by means of countenances of different types.

It is possible to increase the amount of some actions with the ball by players by countenancing a player or a team for performing these actions.

For example, conditions of a drill may suggest shots on goal, performed either by a foot and a head, yet, to countenance shots with a head exactly, any header may count as one goal, and a goal scored with a head – as three.

To stimulate players to finish off the ball into the net, a goal scored in such a manner may count as two.

4. Imposition of restrictions for some actions with the ball.

Restrictions for performing certain actions with the ball allow to increase the amount of repeats of those techniques or technical elements, which training is the main object of a certain drill. They may be imposed:

– for a number of passes to each other by players from one team, performing passes from players to goalkeeper, time of possession, which allows to increase the number of shots on goal;

– for putting the ball into play by goalkeepers in a certain way, performing attacking actions by players through certain area of the playing ground and in a certain way;

– for number of touches by each players, which allows to adjust the volume of individual actions with the ball; for example, a restriction for a play in one and two touches forces players to handle the ball and move with it quickly.

5. Observance of certain soccer rules.

Depending on desired goals, certain soccer rules may or may not be observed in gaming drills with the contiguous goals, such as committing offsides and corners and throw-ins.

6. Using reserve balls.

Certain number of reserve balls, which are initially placed in both goals and put into play by goalkeepers, when a playing ball leaves the drill area far, may be used to increase the volume of players' actions with the ball and vary the intensity of a task performance by them.

For example, availability of 8 reserve balls (four in each goal) nearly always provides the maximum intensity of players' actions during one on one game for one minute.

Taking into account the specifics in the technique of attacking actions in the 18-yard box in matches of teams of high qualification, patterns of goalscoring in soccer and transition of fitness in speed and precision of actions with the ball, there are six sections of gaming drills with the contiguous goals for perfection of the play technique in the 18-yard box with finishing of attacking actions with shots on goal with a foot.

While having similarities in the context of conditions of players' actions, drills from each section differ in the fact that they suggest performance of certain attacking actions with the ball in the 18-yard box to a greater extent:

– only individual actions;
– shots on goal in conditions of the congestion of players;
– shots on goal with a first touch;
– timely passes and a quick first touch;
– obligatory movements with the ball;
– delivery of the ball at the shooting position while abiding the offside.

Soccer. Training the «game episodes technique», beginning from coming over the ball in open play

It is necessary to note that in gaming drills with the contiguous goals for perfection of the play technique in the 18-yard box players, in contradiction to certain attacking actions, are under the natural necessity to perform (train) certain defensive actions, which, in their turn, differ from defensive actions beyond the 18-yard box.

Following are examples of gaming drills with the contiguous goals for perfection of the «game episodes technique» in the 18-yard box in case of performing of a finishing shot on goal with a foot.

Drills suggesting individual actions only

Task 1	
Task description	Requirements for task performance quality
One on one play providing that the ball is put into play by goalkeepers across the pitch surface. Pitch size: 10 meters wide, 10 meters long. 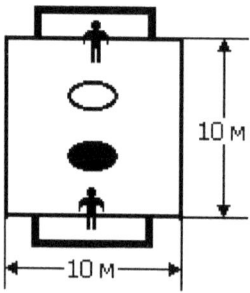 Goalkeepers put the ball into play after catching it or when it crosses the goal-line and sidelines. Corners are not awarded. Offsides are not given. Players are permitted to pass the ball to goalkeepers only when putting it into play after fouls. Goal scored at the rebound counts as two. Play time in one repeat – 1 minutes. **Variant:** goals are dislocated relative to each other every which way along the goal-line	– goalkeepers should put the ball into play without a delay; – players should act as intensively as possible; – players should handle the ball quickly, and especially fast perform the strike motion while shooting on goal; – players should perform shots on goal from any, even inconvenient positions; – players should try to use every opportunity to finish off the ball into the net; – while performing shots on goal, players should try to send the ball into the area of the goal, unprotected by the goalkeeper, every time

Task 2	
Task description	Requirements for task performance quality
One on one play providing that the ball is put into play by goalkeepers with a bounce off the pitch surface. Pitch size: 10 meters wide, 10 meters long. 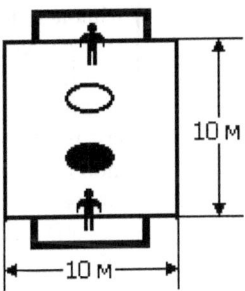 Goalkeepers put the ball into play after catching it or when it crosses the goal-line and sidelines with a bounce off the pitch surface obligingly. Players are permitted to perform shots on goal on the ball that is on the pitch surface and bouncing off it. A goal scored with a strike on the ball in the air counts as two. Players are prohibited from blocking a shot with a highly-raised foot when an opponent shoots on goal on the ball in the air. Corners are not awarded. Offsides are not given. Players are permitted to pass the ball to goalkeepers only when putting it into play after fouls. Goal scored at the rebound counts as two. Play time in one repeat – 1 minutes	– goalkeepers should put the ball into play without a delay; – players should act as intensively as possible; – players should handle the ball quickly, and especially fast perform the strike motion while shooting on goal; – players should perform shots on goal from any, even inconvenient positions; – players should try to use every opportunity to finish off the ball into the net; – while performing shots on goal, players should try to send the ball into the area of the goal, unprotected by the goalkeeper, every time; – when an opponent shoots on goal with the ball in the air, player should block these shots with their body

Drills suggesting shots on goal with a foot in conditions of the congestion of players

Task 3	
Task description	Requirements for task performance quality
Two on two play with the «neutral» player acting all the time for the attacking team. Pitch size: 15 meters wide, 12 meters long. 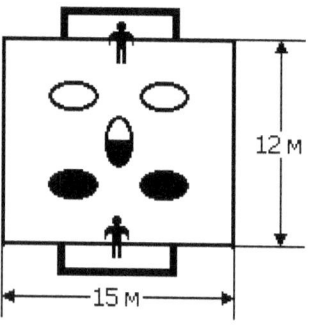 Goalkeepers put the ball into play across the pitch surface after catching it or when it has left the field through the goal-line or sidelines. Number of passes by outfield players during the attack is no more than two. Corners are not awarded. Offsides are not given. Goal scored with a first touch counts as two. Goal scored at the rebound counts as two. Play time in one repeat – 3 minutes. **Variant:** goalkeepers put the ball into play with a bounce off the pitch surface. A goal scored with a strike on the ball in the air counts as two	– goalkeepers should put the ball into play without a delay; – players should handle the ball quickly, and especially fast perform the strike motion while shooting on goal; – players should interact with their partners quickly; – amid space shortage players should look for an opportunity to shoot on goal and not move with the ball to a free space; – players should try to use every opportunity to finish off the ball into the net; – while performing shots on goal, players should try to send the ball into the area of the goal, unprotected by the goalkeeper, every time

Soccer. Training the «game episodes technique», beginning from coming over the ball in open play

Task 2		
	Task description	Requirements for task performance quality
	Two on two play with a «neutral» player acting for the attacking team all the time, providing all players acting in the middle zone. Pitch size: 15 meters wide, 30 meters long. Middle zone 10 meters long and the goal area not far than 5 meters from the goal-line are marked on the pitch. Players are acting in the middle zone all the time. 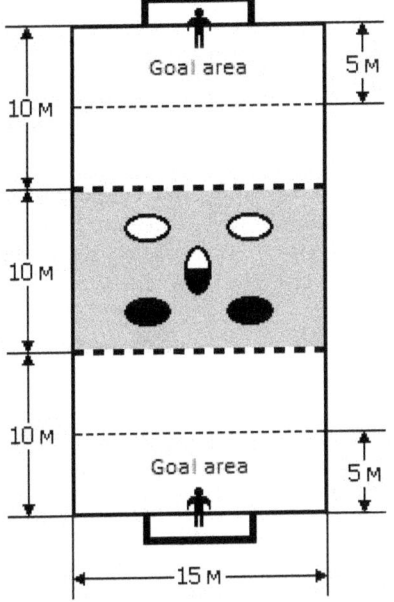 On signal goalkeepers put the ball into play to the middle zone of the pitch from the goal-area after catching it or when it has left the field through the goal-line or sidelines.	– in a short period after a signal for putting the ball into play players should receive the ball from the goalkeeper; – players should use various techniques of opening for receiving the ball from the goalkeeper and partners in the most comfortable position; – while performing passes by the goalkeeper players from the defending team should try to intercept the ball or attack a rival player at reception of the ball, entering into physical contact with him; – goalkeepers and players should pass the ball to the partner timely and precisely, providing him with time for performing a shot on goal; – players should interact with their partners quickly;

Task 2 continuation	
Task description	Requirements for task performance quality
Players from the attacking team try to outplay players from the defending team and shoot on goal from the middle zone. Number of passes by outfield players during the attack is no more than three. Players from the attacking team are permitted to finish off the ball into the net beyond the middle zone. Goal scored in such manner counts as two. Players from the defending team try to prevent attacking players to shoot on goal. Corners are not awarded. Offsides are not given. Goal scored with a first touch counts as two. Play time in one repeat – 5 minutes. **Note.** While alternating the length of zones between the goal-line and the middle zone we may provide conditions for players to shoot on goal from quite longer or shorter distances	– players from the defending team should attack an opponent, who has gained possession of the ball, as fast as possible, forcing him to act amid time and space shortage; – players should handle the ball quickly, and especially fast perform the strike motion while shooting on goal; – players should perform shots on goal from any, even inconvenient positions; – players should try to use every opportunity to finish off the ball into the net; – while performing shots on goal, players should try to send the ball into the area of the goal, unprotected by the goalkeeper, every time

Task 3	
Task description	Requirements for task performance quality
Three on three play. Pitch size: 16 meters wide, 16 meters long. 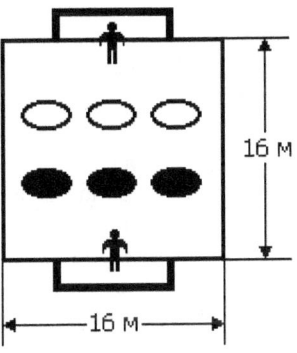 Goalkeepers put the ball into play after catching it or when it crosses the goal-line and sidelines. Number of passes by outfield players during the attack is no more than two. Corners are not awarded. Offsides are not given. Goal scored with a first touch counts as two. Goal scored at the rebound counts as two. Play time in one repeat – 3 minutes. **Variants:** a) the half-way line is marked and offsides are given; b) goalkeepers put the ball into play with a bounce off the pitch surface; c) goals are dislocated relative to each other every which way along the goal-line	– goalkeepers should put the ball into play without a delay; – players should handle the ball quickly, and especially fast perform the strike motion while shooting on goal; – players should interact with their partners quickly; – amid space shortage players should look for an opportunity to shoot on goal and not move with the ball to a free space; – players should perform shots on goal from any, even inconvenient positions; – players should try to use every opportunity to finish off the ball into the net; – while performing shots on goal, players should try to send the ball into the area of the goal, unprotected by the goalkeeper, every time

Task 4	
Task description	Requirements for task performance quality
Three on three play with the «neutral» player acting all the time for the attacking team. Pitch size: 20 meters wide, 16 meters long. 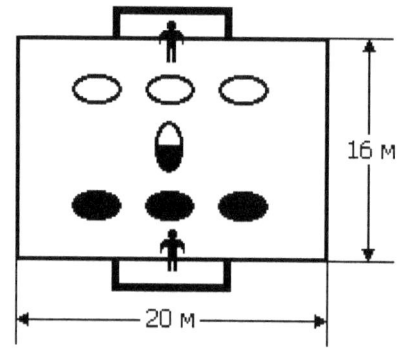 Goalkeepers put the ball into play after catching it or when it crosses the goal-line and sidelines. Number of passes by outfield players during the attack is no more than two. Corners are not awarded. Offsides are not given. Goal scored with a first touch counts as two. Goal scored at the rebound counts as two. Play time in one repeat – 5 minutes. **Variants:** a) goalkeepers put the ball into play with a bounce off the pitch surface; b) goals are dislocated relative to each other every which way along the goal-line	– goalkeepers should put the ball into play without a delay; – players should handle the ball quickly, and especially fast perform the strike motion while shooting on goal; – amid space shortage players should look for an opportunity to shoot on goal and not move with the ball to a free space; – players should perform shots on goal from any, even inconvenient positions; – players should try to use every opportunity to finish off the ball into the net; – while performing shots on goal, players should try to send the ball into the area of the goal, unprotected by the goalkeeper, every time

Drills suggesting shots on goal with a first touch

Task 1	
Task description	Requirements for task performance quality
Three on three play providing that shots on goal are performed with a first touch. Pitch size: 20 meters wide, 16 meters long. 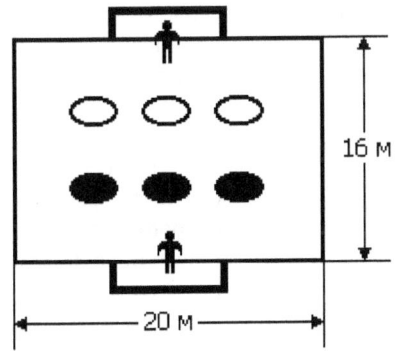 Goalkeepers put the ball into play after catching it or when it crosses the goal-line and sidelines. Shots on goal are performed **with a first touch obligingly.** Number of passes by outfield players during the attack is no more than three. Corners are not awarded. Offsides are not given. Goal scored at the rebound counts as two. Play time in one repeat – 3 minutes	– goalkeepers should put the ball into play without a delay; – players should begin preparative actions for shooting on goal timely relative to the moment when their partner with the ball is ready to perform a pass; – players should perform passes for shooting on goal with a maximum precision; – players should try to use every opportunity to finish off the ball into the net; – while performing shots on goal, players should try to send the ball into the area of the goal, unprotected by the goalkeeper, every time

Task 2	
Task description	Requirements for task performance quality
Three on three play with a «neutral» player acting for the attacking team all the time providing shooting on goal with a first touch. Pitch size: 30 meters wide, 20 meters long. Three zones are marked on the pitch: two lateral 6 meters wide each and the middle 18 meters wide. 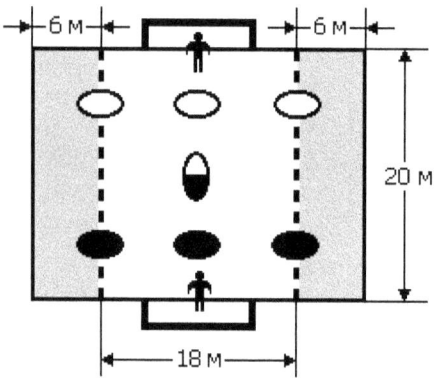 Goalkeepers put the ball into play to lateral zones after catching it or when it crosses the goal-line and sidelines. Shots on goal are performed **from the middle zone with a first touch obligingly** after a pass from the lateral zone. Number of passes by outfield players during the attack is no more than three. Corners are not awarded. Offsides are not given. Goal scored at the rebound counts as two. Play time in one repeat – 5 minutes	– goalkeepers should put the ball into play without a delay; – players should begin preparative actions for shooting on goal timely relative to the moment when their partner with the ball is ready to perform a pass; – players should perform passes for shooting on goal with a maximum precision; – players should perform shots on goal from any, even inconvenient positions; – players should try to use every opportunity to finish off the ball into the net; – while performing shots on goal, players should try to send the ball into the area of the goal, unprotected by the goalkeeper, every time

Task 3		
	Task description	Requirements for task performance quality
	Four on four play providing that shots on goal are performed with a first or a second touch. Pitch size: 16 meters wide, 16 meters long. 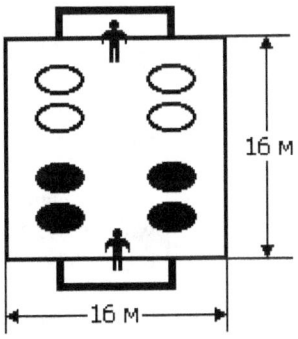 Goalkeepers put the ball into play after catching it or when it crosses the goal-line and sidelines with a mounted trajectory obligingly. Players from the attacking team try to pass the ball with a head or a foot to partners for shooting on goal **with a first touch of a foot or a head.** Goal scored in such manner counts as three. Players are permitted to shoot on goal with a second touch. Corners are not awarded. Offsides are not given. Players are permitted to pass the ball to goalkeepers. Goal scored at the rebound counts as two. Play time in one repeat – 5 minutes	– goalkeepers should put the ball into play without a delay with a mounted trajectory obligingly; – players should try to win the ball after putting into the play by the goalkeepers with a mounted trajectory; – players should try to perform passes and shots on goal also with a physical contact with an opponent; – players should shoot on goal with a foot or a head from any, even inconvenient positions; – players should try to use every opportunity to finish off the ball into the net; – while performing shots on goal, players should try to send the ball into the area of the goal, unprotected by the goalkeeper, every time

Drills suggesting obligatory movements with the ball

Task 1	
Task description	Requirements for task performance quality
Two on two play with a «neutral» player acting for the attacking team all the time, providing prohibition of play in one and two touches. Pitch size: 14 meters wide, 18 meters long. 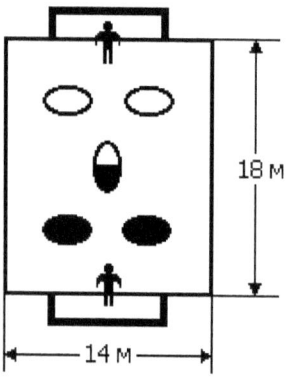 Goalkeepers put the ball into play after catching it or when it crosses the goal-line and sidelines. Players are **prohibited from playing one and two touches,** excluding cases of finishing off the ball into the net. They should handle the ball in a certain situation with the foot they have touched the ball first in this situation. Number of passes by outfield players during the attack is no more than two. Corners are not awarded. Offsides are not given. Play time in one repeat – 3 minutes	– goalkeepers should put the ball into play without a delay; – players should receive the ball with the drifting; – while receiving the ball players should try to powerfully switch into the game, moving with it towards the opponent's goal; – players should bravely try to beat an opponent; – players should perform shots on goal from any, even inconvenient positions; – players should try to use every opportunity to finish off the ball into the net; – while performing shots on goal, players should try to send the ball into the area of the goal, unprotected by the goalkeeper, every time

Task 2	
Task description	Requirements for task performance quality
Two on two play with a «neutral» player acting for the attacking team all the time, providing shooting on goal from the defending zone and prohibition of play in one and two touches. Pitch size: 20 meters wide, 16 meters long. Half-way line dividing the pitch into attacking and defensive zones is marked. 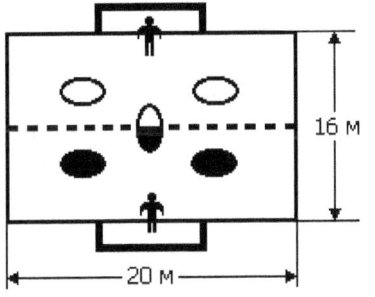 Goalkeepers put the ball into play to their team defensive zone after catching it or when it crosses the goal-line and sidelines. Players are **prohibited to play in one and two touches**. They should handle the ball with foot they have touched the ball for the first time in the certain situation, and perform shots on goal only from the defensive zone. Number of passes by outfield players during the attack is no more than two. Players are permitted to finish off the ball into the net in the attacking zone. Corners are not awarded. Play time in one repeat – 3 minutes	– goalkeepers should put the ball into play without a delay; – players should receive the ball with the drifting; – while receiving the ball players should try to powerfully switch into the game, moving with it towards the sideline; – players should bravely try to beat an opponent; – players should perform shots on goal from any, even inconvenient positions; – players should try to use every opportunity to finish off the ball into the net; – while performing shots on goal, players should try to send the ball into the area of the goal, unprotected by the goalkeeper, every time

Drills suggesting timely passes for shooting on goal

Task 1	
Task description	Requirements for task performance quality
Three on three play providing two players acting in the defensive zone and one in the attacking zone all the time. Pitch size: 15 meters wide, 18 meters long. Three zones are marked on the pitch: attacking and defensive 7 meters long each and the middle 4 meters long. In each team two players act in their team defensive zone, and one – in the attacking zone all the time. Players are prohibited from moving from zone to zone. 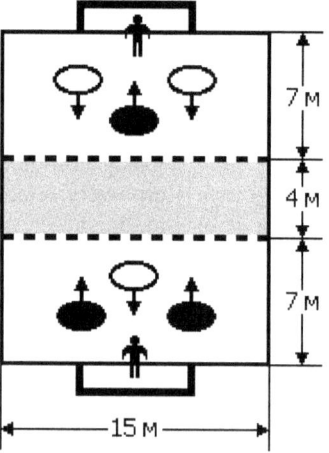 Goalkeepers put the ball into play to their team defensive zone after catching it or when it crosses the goal-line and sidelines.	– goalkeepers should put the ball into play without a delay; – a player from the defending team acting in the opponents' defensive zone should attack a rival player to whom the ball is passed as quick as possible, forcing him to act amid time and space shortage; – players should pass the ball to the partner timely and precisely, providing him with time for performing a shot on goal; – player from the attacking team, acting in the attacking zone, should reduce the visibility for the goalkeeper and change the direction of the ball when his partners shoot on goal;

Soccer. Training the «game episodes technique», beginning from coming over the ball in open play

Task 1 continuation	
Task description	Requirements for task performance quality
Two players from the attacking team acting in the defensive zone try to outplay a player from the defending team and shoot on goal from this zone. Number of passes by outfield players during the attack is no more than two. Player from the attacking team, acting in the attacking zone, tries to reduce the visibility for the goalkeeper, change the direction of the ball to the goal and finish off the ball into the net. Player from the defending team, acting in the opponent's defensive zone, tries to tackle the ball and pass it to his partners in his team defensive zone. Corners are not awarded. Offsides are not given. Goal scored with a first touch counts as two. Goal scored at the rebound counts as two. Play time in one repeat – 5 minutes. **Variants:** a) a player from the defending team, acting in the opponents' defensive zone, is permitted to shoot on goal in case of tackling; b) players from the attacking team, acting in the defensive zone, are permitted to shot on goal from the middle zone while diving	– players should handle the ball quickly, and especially fast perform the strike motion while shooting on goal; – players should perform shots on goal from any, even inconvenient positions; – attacking players should shoot on goal also with a first touch; – a player from the attacking team, acting in the attacking zone, should try to use every opportunity to finish off the ball into the net; – while performing shots on goal, players should try to send the ball into the area of the goal, unprotected by the goalkeeper, every time

Task 2	
Task description	Requirements for task performance quality
Four attacking players on two defending players in two zones, positioned at some distance from each other, providing performing passes from zone to zone while standing still and on course of local movements. Two zones 10 meters wide and 15 meters long are marked on the pitch opposite to each other with long sides at 5 meters. Goals are mounted on the opposite short sides of different zones. Two attacking and one defending player act in each zone all the time. Players are prohibited from moving from zone to zone. 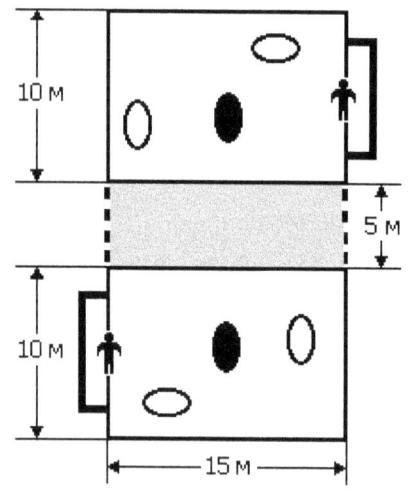 Goalkeepers put the ball into play to the zone where they protect their goal after catching it or when it leaves this area.	– goalkeepers should put the ball into play without a delay; – defending players should try to intercept the ball or attack an opponent at reception of the ball, entering into physical contact with him; – attacking players, acting in the same zone, should pass the ball to each other timely and precisely, providing the partner with time for performing a pass into the opposite zone; – defending players should attack an opponent, who has gained possession of the ball, as fast as possible, forcing him to act amid time and space shortage; – having received the ball from the other zone, attacking players should try to quickly finish the attack with a shot on goal;

Soccer. Training the «game episodes technique», beginning from coming over the ball in open play

Task 2 continuation	
Task description	Requirements for task performance quality
Two attacking players try to pass the ball into the opposite zone for their partners to shoot on goal. Number of passes to each other by attacking players who have received the ball from the goalkeeper before sending it to the opposite zone is no more than two. Number of passes to each other by attacking players who have received the ball from the opposite zone before shooting on goal is no more than two. One of defending players tries to prevent attacking players from passing into the opposite zone, while the another – to shoot on goal. The task for four attacking players is to score as much goals as possible in a definite time. **Offsides are given.** Goal scored with a first touch counts as two. Goal scored at the rebound counts as two. **Variants:** a) goals are mounted opposite to each other on the opposite long sides of different zones; b) passes from zone to zone are performed with the mounted trajectory obligingly	– attacking players, positioned in different zones, should act simultaneously while trying to deliver the ball from zone to zone; – players should handle the ball quickly, and especially fast perform the strike motion while shooting on goal; – players should perform shots on goal from any, even inconvenient positions; – players should try to use every opportunity to finish off the ball into the net; – while performing shots on goal, players should try to send the ball into the area of the goal, unprotected by the goalkeeper, every time

Task 3	
Task description	Requirements for task performance quality
Four attacking players on two defending players in two zones, positioned at some distance from each other, providing performing passes from zone to zone on course of local movements. Two zones 10 meters wide and 18 meters long are marked on the pitch with long sides opposite to each other 5 meters apart. Goal-areas are marked in each zone no further than 5 meters from the goal-line. Goals are mounted on the opposite short sides of different zones. Two attacking and one defending player act in each zone all the time. Players are prohibited from moving from zone to zone. 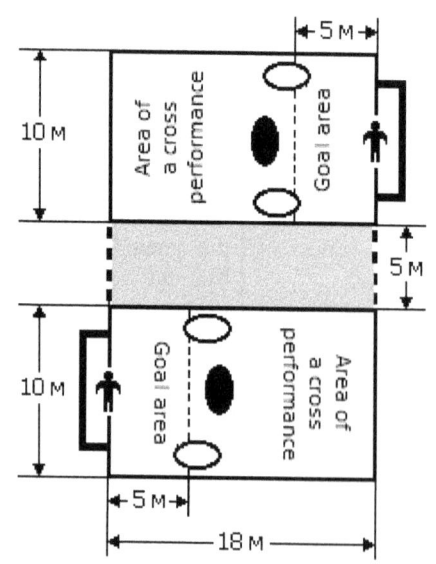	– goalkeepers should put the ball into play without a delay; – defending players should try to intercept the ball or attack an opponent at reception of the ball, entering into physical contact with him; – having received the ball from the goalkeeper, attacking players should try to deliver it to the «area of a cross performance» quickly and pass it into the opposite zone; – attacking players, acting in the same zone, should pass the ball to each other timely and precisely, providing the partner with time for performing a pass into the opposite zone; – having received the ball from the other zone, attacking players should try to quickly finish the attack with a shot on goal;

Soccer. Training the «game episodes technique», beginning from coming over the ball in open play

Task 3 continuation

Task description	Requirements for task performance quality
Goalkeepers put the ball into play inside the goal-area in the zone where they protect their goal after catching it or when it leaves this area. Two attacking players try to deliver the ball from the goal-area to the «area of a cross performance» and pass the ball into the opposite zone for partners to shoot o goal. Number of passes to each other by attacking players who have received the ball from the goalkeeper before sending it to the opposite zone is no more than two. Number of passes to each other by attacking players who have received the ball from the opposite zone before shooting on goal is no more than two. One of defending players tries to prevent attacking players from passing into the opposite zone, while the another – to shoot on goal. While putting the ball into play by the goalkeeper a defending player, acting in this zone, is positioned inside the goal-area. The task for four attacking players is to score as much goals as possible in a definite time. **Offsides are given.** Goal scored with a first touch counts as two. Goal scored at the rebound counts as two	– attacking players, positioned in different zones, should act simultaneously while trying to deliver the ball from zone to zone; – defending players should attack an opponent, who has gained possession of the ball, as fast as possible, forcing him to act amid time and space shortage; – players should perform shots on goal from any, even inconvenient positions; – players should try to use every opportunity to finish off the ball into the net; – while performing shots on goal, players should try to send the ball into the area of the goal, unprotected by the goalkeeper, every time

Task 4	
Task description	Requirements for task performance quality
Three on three play with a «neutral» player acting for the attacking team all the time, providing all players are initially positioned in the middle zone of the pitch. Pitch size: 20 meters wide, 25 meters long. Three zones are marked on the pitch: attacking and defensive 10 meters long each and the middle 5 meters long. Goal-areas are marked in defensive and attacking zones no further than 5 meters from the goal-line. Players are initially positioned in the middle zone. 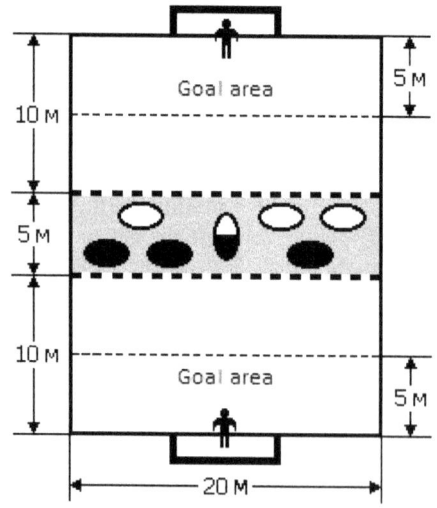 On signal goalkeepers put the ball into play to the middle zone of the pitch from the goal-area after catching it or when it has left the field through the goal-line or sidelines.	– in a short period after a signal for putting the ball into play players should receive the ball from the goalkeeper; – players should use various techniques of opening for receiving the ball from the goalkeeper and partners in the most comfortable position; – while performing passes by the goalkeeper players from the defending team should try to intercept the ball or attack a rival player at reception of the ball, entering into physical contact with him; – goalkeepers and players should pass the ball to the partner timely and precisely, providing him with time for performing a shot on goal; – players should interact with each other quickly;

Soccer. Training the «game episodes technique», beginning from coming over the ball in open play

Task 4 continuation	
Task description	Requirements for task performance quality
Players from the attacking team try to beat players from the defending team and shoot on goal from the middle or attacking zone. Number of passes by outfield players during the attack is no more than three. Players from the defending team try to prevent players from the attacking team to shoot on goal and to knock the ball out of the middle and attacking zone. In the event of the attack finishing, catching the ball by the goalkeeper or clearance by players from the defending team beyond the middle zone and their defensive zone all players occupy starting positions in the middle zone. Corners are not awarded. **Offsides are given in the attacking zone.** Goal scored with a first touch counts as two. Goal scored at the rebound counts as two. Play time in one repeat – 10 minutes. **Variants:** a) goals are dislocated relative to each other every which way along the goal-line; b) goalkeepers' functions are performed by outfield players, who are permitted to protect the goal with any body part except for arms; c) four on four play	– players from the defending team should attack an opponent, who has gained possession of the ball, as fast as possible, forcing him to act amid time and space shortage; – players should handle the ball quickly, and especially fast perform the strike motion while shooting on goal; – players should perform shots on goal from any, even inconvenient positions; – players should try to use every opportunity to finish off the ball into the net; – while performing shots on goal, players should try to send the ball into the area of the goal, unprotected by the goalkeeper, every time

Drills suggesting the delivery of the ball at the shooting position while abiding the offside

Task 1	
Task description	Requirements for task performance quality
Three on three play with a «neutral» player acting for the attacking team all the time providing crossing the half-way line by a pass. Pitch size: 20 meters wide, 25 meters long. The half-way line, dividing the pitch in attacking and defensive zones, is marked. 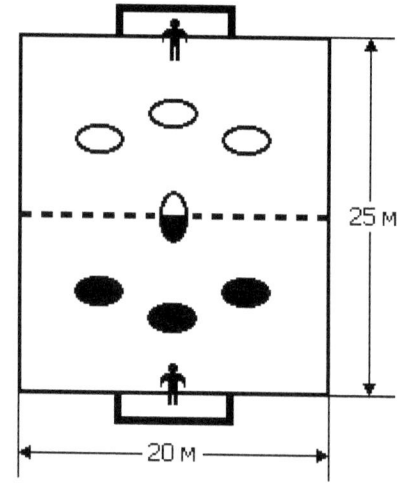 Goalkeepers put the ball into play to their team defensive zone after catching it or when it crosses the goal-line and sidelines. Players from the attacking team try to deliver the ball from the defensive into the attacking zone by means of a pass across the half-way line and to shoot on goal from this zone.	– goalkeepers should put the ball into play without a delay; – players from the attacking team should try to deliver the ball into the attacking zone quickly and shoot on goal; – players from the attacking team should timely open to receive the ball while performing passes from the defensive into the attacking zone; – players should handle the ball quickly, and especially fast perform the strike motion while shooting on goal; – players from the defending team should attack a player, who has gained possession of the ball, as fast as possible, forcing him to act amid time shortage;

Soccer. Training the «game episodes technique», beginning from coming over the ball in open play

Task 1 continuation	
Task description	Requirements for task performance quality
Number of passes by outfield players during the attack is no more than three. Number of touches by each player is not limited. Players from the defending team try to prevent players from the attacking team from delivering the ball into the attacking zone and shoot on goal while positioning in the opponents' defensive zone when their goalkeeper puts the ball into play. Corners are not awarded. **Offsides are given.** Goal scored with a first touch counts as two. Goal scored at the rebound counts as two. Play time in one repeat – 5 minutes	– players should try to use every opportunity to finish off the ball into the net; – while performing shots on goal, players should try to send the ball into the area of the goal, unprotected by the goalkeeper, every time

Task 2	
Task description	Requirements for task performance quality
Three on three play with a «neutral» player acting for the attacking team all the time providing crossing the half-way line with dribbling. Pitch size: 20 meters wide, 25 meters long. The half-way line, dividing the pitch in attacking and defensive zones, is marked. 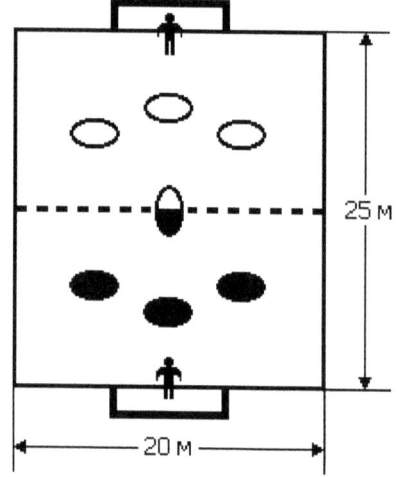 Goalkeepers put the ball into play to their team defensive zone after catching it or when it crosses the goal-line and sidelines. Players from the attacking team try to deliver the ball from the defensive into the attacking zone by means of dribbling across the half-way line and to shoot on goal from this zone. Number of passes by outfield players during the attack is no more than two.	– goalkeepers should put the ball into play without a delay; – players from the attacking team should try to deliver the ball into the attacking zone quickly and shoot on goal; – while receiving the ball players should try to powerfully switch into the game, moving with it at sufficiently long distance; – players should cross the half-way line with the ball, as well as with beating an opponent; – players should handle the ball quickly, and especially fast perform the strike motion while shooting on goal; – players from the defending team should attack a player, who has gained possession of the ball, as fast as possible, forcing him to act amid time shortage;

Soccer. Training the «game episodes technique», beginning from coming over the ball in open play

Task 2 continuation	
Task description	Requirements for task performance quality
Number of touches by each player is not limited. Players from the defending team try to prevent players from the attacking team from delivering the ball into the attacking zone and shoot on goal while positioning in the opponents' defensive zone when their goalkeeper puts the ball into play. Corners are not awarded. **Offsides are given.** Goal scored with a first touch counts as two. Goal scored at the rebound counts as two. Play time in one repeat – 5 minutes	– players should try to use every opportunity to finish off the ball into the net; – while performing shots on goal, players should try to send the ball into the area of the goal, unprotected by the goalkeeper, every time

Training the game technique while finishing the attacking actions with a header

Kicks on the ball with a head are performed in any area of the pitch, though the ability to play with a head takes on particular importance in the 18-yard box. Rudely each fourth goal of whose scored in the 18-yard box (excluding goals scored from the penalty spot) is scored with a head.

The main goals for improving the technique of head-playing are:

– reaching the maximum level of proficiency in a basic for a certain player way of shooting on goal or passing with a head (perfection of a go-to technique);

– elimination of possible certain shortcomings in head-playing.

While the way of performing shots in the context of using one or another mechanism of shooting (with an active body movement, a shake, by means of creating a large impact weight) is generally defined in facilitated conditions while learning the technique of kicking the ball with a head, drills for perfection of the head-playing technique in the 18-yard box suggest performing passes and shots on goals in conditions, simulating the real game episodes.

To play with a head well it is necessary to play with it a lot. However, due to the specificity of the head-playing performance there is a contradiction between the volume of cases of shooting on goal and passes with a head by attacking players in drills and specialization of drills, which increases as the training conditions come close to those of competitive matches. Even the passive resistance of defending players sufficiently affects the number of touches by a head by attacking players.

A role of a player passing the ball to his partners for shooting with a head also increases along with the increase of the drills specialization.

Large volumes of cases of head-playing may be achieved by players' motivation for such play, which is developed in childhood, and by means of drills setup.

A choice of areas from which shots on goal with a head and passes for such shots are performed is essential for constructing drills for perfection of the head-playing technique inside the 18-yard box. Passes for shooting on goal with a head should be performed over the entire range of possible directions of the ball sending inside of areas, from which passes, resulting in goalscoring with a head, are performed and goals with a head are scored in competitive matches (see fig. 7).

A position of a player preparing to shoot with a head relative to the opponent's goal (side or face to the goal) also has to be noted. This is due to the fact that it is more comfortable to shoot in an active manner (with an evident striking action) while being face to the goal. It is less comfortable to actively shoot with a head while being side to the goal, and so in these cases (either in supporting and non-supporting position) player generally change the direction of the ball with a quick movement of a head.

It is preferable for players to train the widest possible range of situations occurring in competitive matches, in the context of direction combinations of passes for shooting with a head and sending the ball into the net in various positions.

Shots on goal with a head may be performed without and with the active counterwork of an opponent (to the extent of a physical contact) at the moment of touching the ball.

When the ball is sent to a player standing still, his head is a decent mark, facilitating the performance of an accurate pass.

In case a player should supposedly shoot with a head in motion, the ball should be sent to the point at some distance from this player. This is more complicated for a passing player, and the number of inaccurate passes increases in these cases consequently.

One of methodological techniques for facilitating actions of players, passing the ball to moving partners, and thus for increasing the volume of cases of performing shots with a head, is the employment of additional landmarks, spotting the area the ball should be sent into.

A function of a landmark may be fulfilled by a player position in a certain point. In this case the ball is sent at him with an intended trajectory so that an attacking player who knows in which point he will meet the ball with a head in advance could either perform a shot after the ball flies over this player or play a lead.

Fulfilling a function of a landmark by one of players from the attacking team may be also used in competitive matches while performing set-pieces: corners, direct and indirect free kicks, throw-ins.

There are three kinds of drills developed for training the «game episodes technique», beginning from coming over the ball in open play by players, when attacking actions are finished with shot on goal with a head and passes with a head for shooting on goal:

– with a regular beginning and regular finishing of players' of actions with the ball;

– with a regular beginning and variative finishing of players' of actions with the ball;

– with a variative beginning and variative finishing of players' of actions with the ball.

Following are examples of drills for perfection of the head-playing technique inside the 18-yard box by players.

Drills with a regular beginning and regular finishing of players' of actions with the ball

Task 1	
Task description	Requirements for task performance quality
Players' initial position, sequence of their actions and directions of movement An attacking player is positioned in the limited space sideways to the goal. 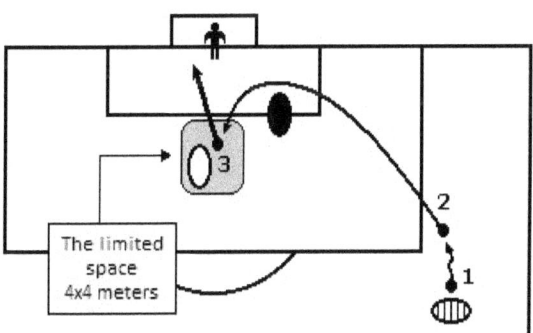 A partner of an attacking player moves with the ball several meters towards the goal-line and sends the ball to an attacking player into the limited space with a mounted trajectory above a defending player. An attacking player shoots on goal with a head in supporting position or in a jump. **Variants:** a) an attacking player is positioned face to the goal in the initial position; b) points of marking of the limited space and players' initial position are varied;	– a partner of an attacking player should perform passes while moving; – a partner of an attacking player should direct the ball with the lowest trajectory possible, yet so that it flew above a defending player; – an attacking player should try to send the ball with a head into the area of the goal, unprotected by the goalkeeper, every time

Task 1 continuation	
Task description	Requirements for task performance quality

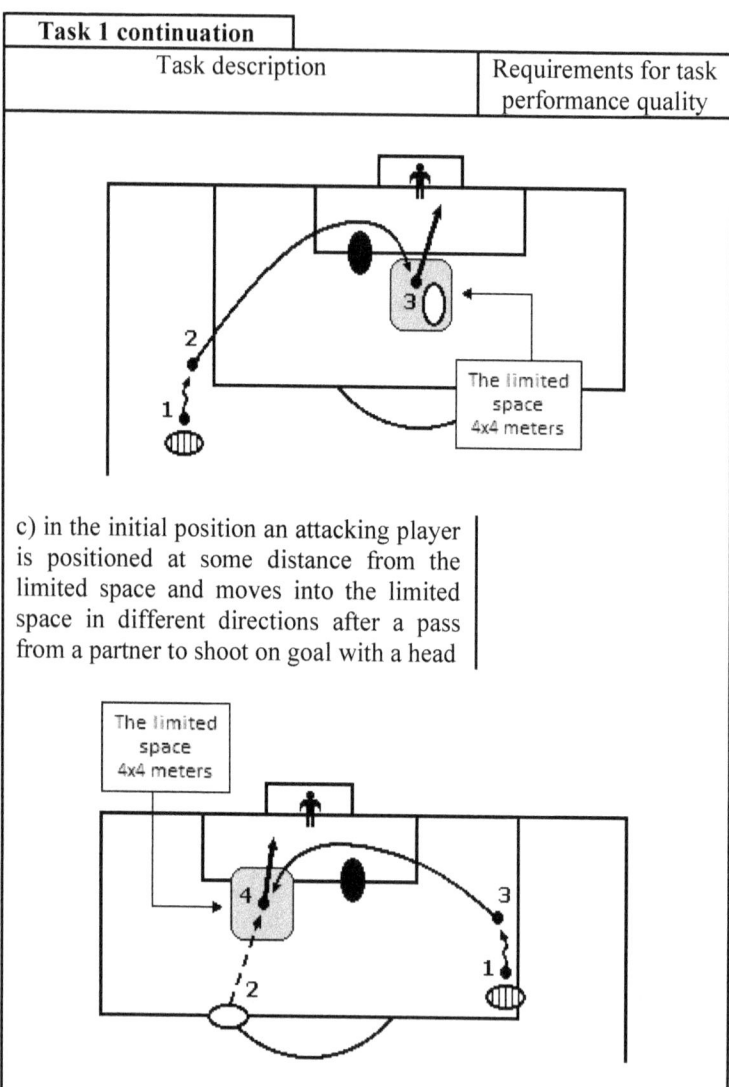

c) in the initial position an attacking player is positioned at some distance from the limited space and moves into the limited space in different directions after a pass from a partner to shoot on goal with a head

Soccer. Training the «game episodes technique», beginning from coming over the ball in open play

Task 2	
Task description	Requirements for task performance quality
Players' initial position, sequence of their actions and directions of movement	– a partner of an attacking player should perform passes while moving;

[Diagram: The limited space 6x6 meters]

A partner of an attacking player moves with the ball several meters towards the goal-line and sends the ball to an attacking player into the limited space with a high mounted trajectory above the mannequine, designating a defending player. An attacking player shoots on goal with a head in a jump with a contact with a defending player. A defending player passively confronts an attacking player in supporting position. **Variants:** a) points of marking of the limited space and players' initial position are varied; c) in the initial position an attacking player is positioned at some distance from the limited space and moves into the limited space in different directions after a pass from a partner to shoot on goal with a head	– an attacking player should shoot on goal with a head with a physical contact with an opponent; – a defending player should confront an attacking player in such manner that the latter could shoot on goal nonetheless; – an attacking player should try to send the ball with a head into the area of the goal, unprotected by the goalkeeper, every time

Task 2 continuation	
Task description	Requirements for task performance quality

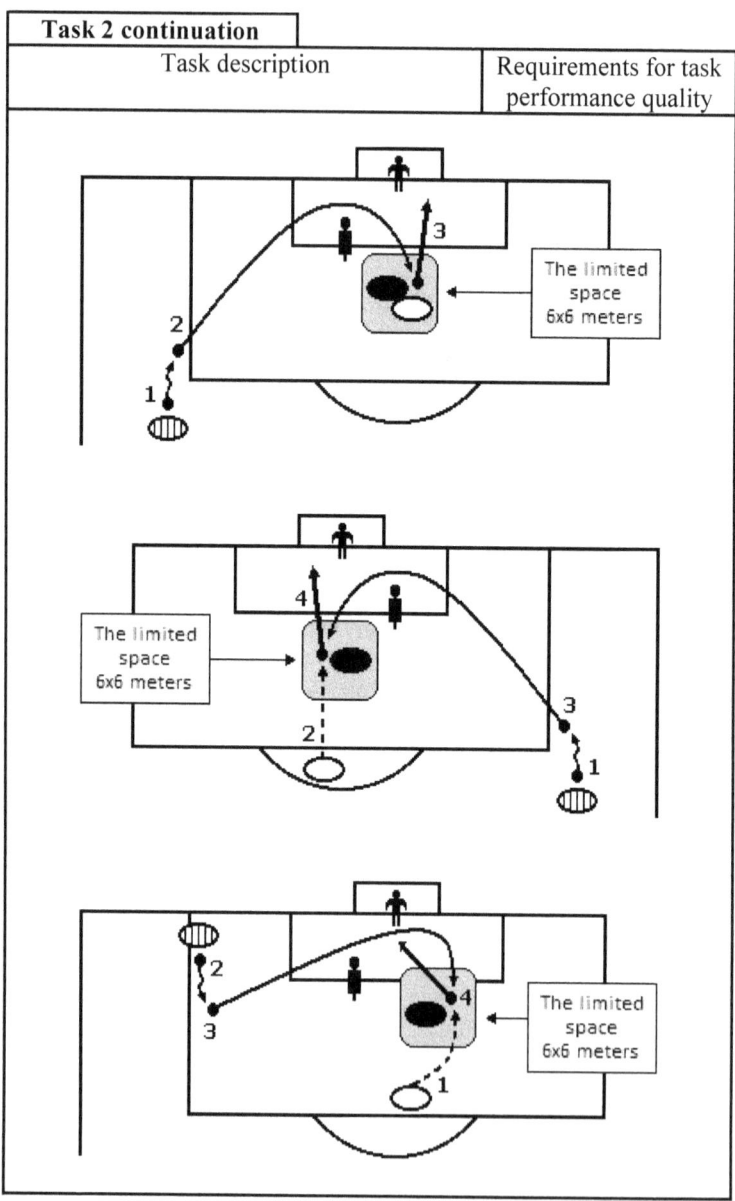

Soccer. Training the «game episodes technique», beginning from coming over the ball in open play

Task 3		
	Task description	Requirements for task performance quality
	Players' initial position, sequence of their actions and directions of movement A defending player is positioned very close to an attacking player.	– a partner of an attacking player should perform passes while moving;

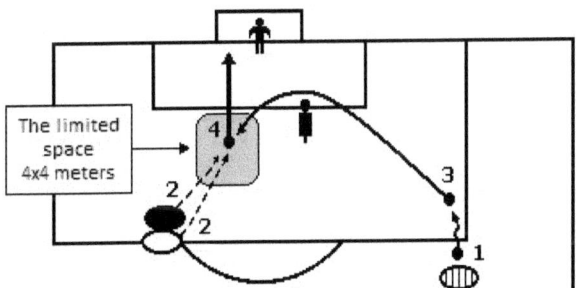

A partner of an attacking player moves with the ball several meters towards the goal-line and sends the ball to an attacking player into the limited space with a mounted trajectory above the mannequin, designating a defending player. An attacking player moves into the limited space and shoots on goal with a head **with a contact with a defending player.** A defending player begins to move into the limited space alongside with an attacking player and passively confronts him, being in a contact with him all the time. **Variant:** points of marking of the limited space and players' initial position are varied	– an attacking player should begin to move into the limited space timely relative to the moment of the pass performing by a partner; – an attacking player should shoot on goal with a head with a physical contact with an opponent; – a defending player should confront an attacking player in such manner that the latter could shoot on goal nonetheless;

Task 3 continuation	
Task description	Requirements for task performance quality
	– an attacking player should try to send the ball with a head into the area of the goal, unprotected by the goalkeeper, every time

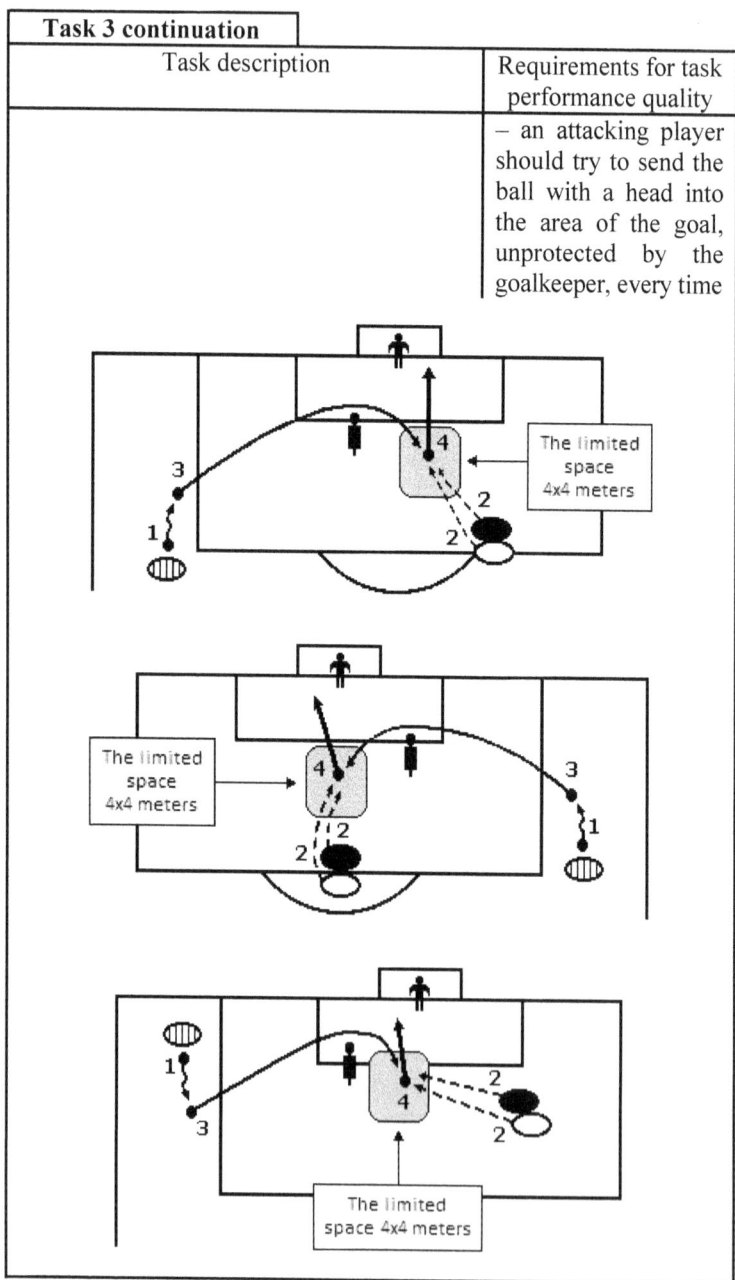

Task 4	
Task description	Requirements for task performance quality
Players' initial position, sequence of their actions and directions of movement A defending player is positioned at the side of the limited space, distant relative to an attacking player's partner.	– a partner of an attacking player should perform passes while moving;
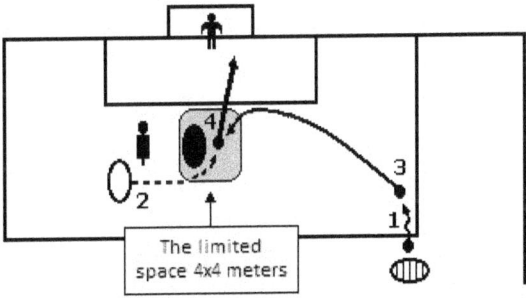	
A partner of an attacking player moves with the ball several meters from the goal-line and sends the ball into the limited space to a defending player with a low mounted trajectory. An attacking player moves into the limited space and shoots on goal with a head **in close vicinity to a defending player from the side of a pass performance by a partner.** A defending player is permitted to play the ball with a head **in static position only.** **Variant:** points of marking of the limited space and players' initial position are varied	– an attacking player should begin to move into the limited space timely relative to the moment of the pass performing by a partner; – an attacking player should shoot on goal with a head, obligingly advancing a defending player; – a defending player should confront an attacking player in such manner that the latter could shoot on goal nonetheless;

Task 4 continuation	
Task description	Requirements for task performance quality
	– an attacking player should try to send the ball with a head into the area of the goal, unprotected by the goalkeeper, every time

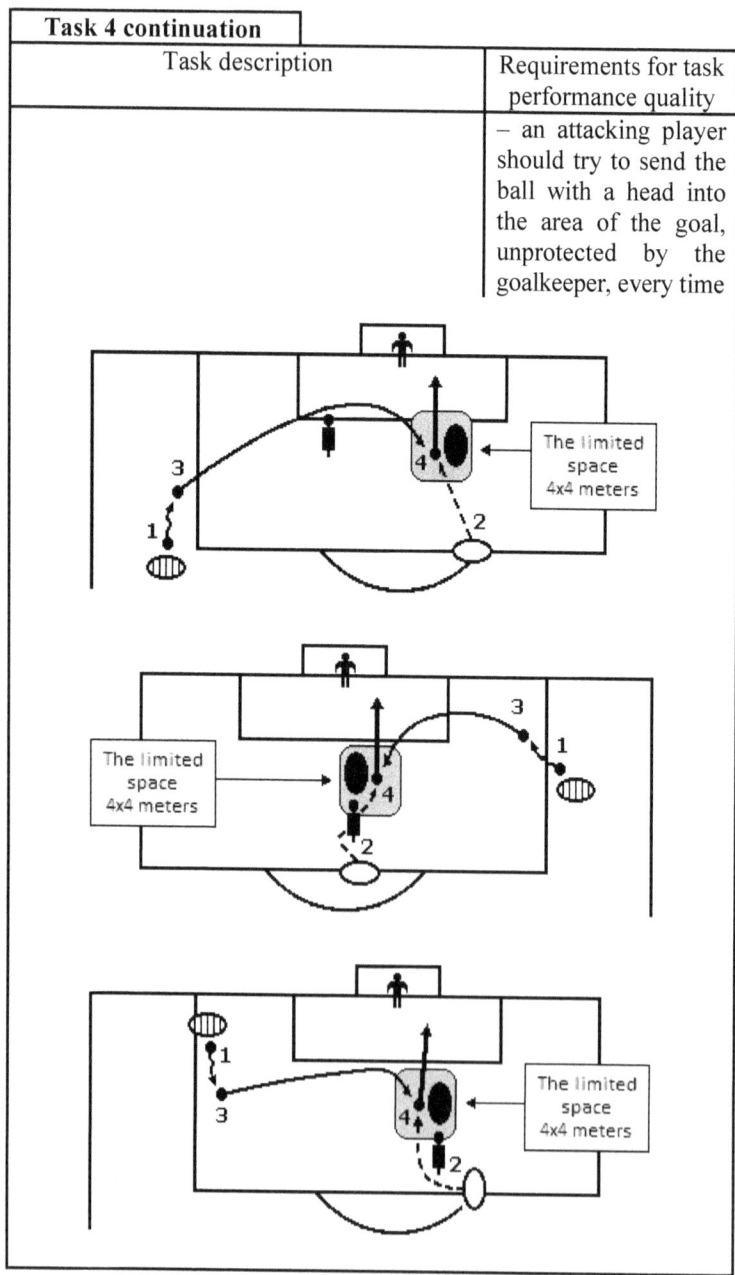

Drills with a regular beginning and variative finishing of players' of actions with the ball

Task 1	
Task description	Requirements for task performance quality
Players' initial position, sequence of their actions and directions of movement	– a partner of attacking players should perform passes while moving;
A partner of attacking players moves with the ball several meters towards the goal-line and sends the ball into the limited space to one of attacking player with a high mounted trajectory. An attacking player shoots on goal with a head (variant A) or performs a pass by a head to the second attacking player for shooting on goal with a head or a foot from the limited space with a first touch (variant B). A defending player **passively confronts** attacking players **in supporting position**. **Variants:** a) points of marking of the limited space and players' initial position are varied;	– attacking players should try to perform shots on goal or passes with a head for a following shot on goal depending on the trajectory of the ball and actions of a defending player; – attacking players should shoot on goal and pass with a head also with a physical contact with an opponent;

Task 1 continuation	
Task description	Requirements for task performance quality
b) in the initial position attacking players are positioned at some distance from the limited space and move into the limited space in different directions after a pass from a partner to shoot on goal;	– attacking players should try to send the ball with a head into the area of the goal, unprotected by the goalkeeper, every time;

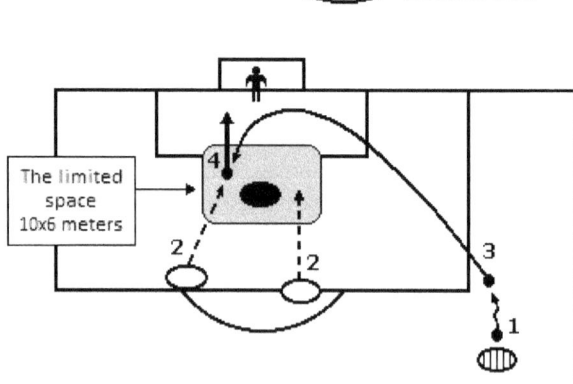

c) a defending player actively confronts attacking players **in supporting position**	– a defending player should confront attacking players in such manner that they were able to shoot on goal or pass with a head for a following shot on goal

Soccer. Training the «game episodes technique», beginning from coming over the ball in open play

Task 2	
Task description	Requirements for task performance quality
Players' initial position, sequence of their actions and directions of movement	– a partner of attacking players should perform passes while moving;

[Diagram: The limited space 10x6 meters, showing players A, B, C with positions 3, 4, 4 and external players 1, 2 with ball]

A partner of attacking players moves with the ball several meters towards the goal-line and sends the ball into the limited space to one of attacking player with a high mounted trajectory. An attacking player shoots on goal with a head (variant A) or performs a pass by a head to another attacking player for shooting on goal with a head or a foot from the limited space with a first touch (variants B and C). A defending player **actively confronts** attacking players. **Variants:** a) points of marking of the limited space and players' initial position are varied; b) in the initial position attacking players are positioned at some distance from the limited space and move into the limited space in different directions after a pass from a partner to shoot on goal	– attacking players should try to perform shots on goal or passes with a head for a following shot on goal depending on the trajectory of the ball and actions of a defending player; – attacking players should shoot on goal and pass with a head also with a physical contact with an opponent; – attacking players should perform shots on goal from any, even inconvenient positions;

Task 2 continuation	
Task description	Requirements for task performance quality
	– attacking players should try to send the ball with a head into the area of the goal, unprotected by the goalkeeper, every time

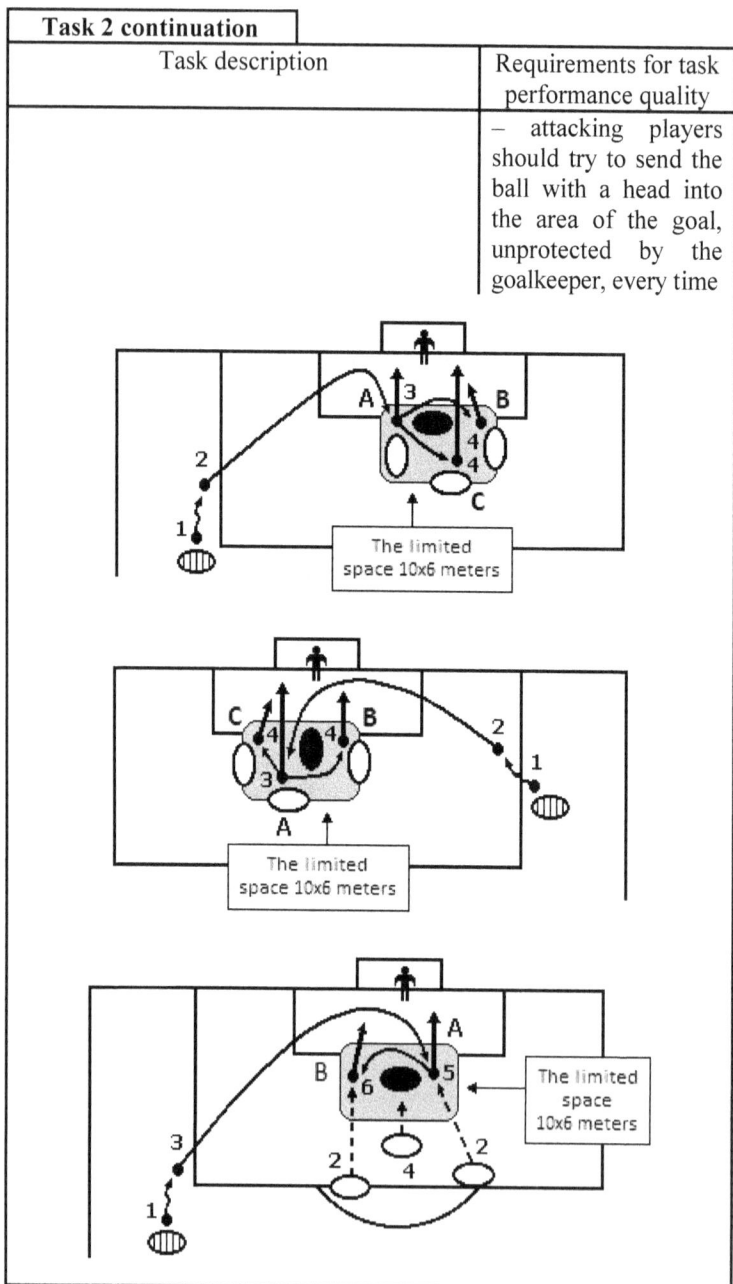

Task 3		
	Task description	Requirements for task performance quality
	Players' initial position, sequence of their actions and directions of movement	– a partner of attacking players should perform passes while moving;
	[Diagram: The limited space 10x10 meters, showing players 1, 2, 3, 4 and goal]	
	A partner of attacking players moves with the ball several meters towards the goal-line and sends the ball into the limited space to one of attacking player with a high mounted trajectory. An attacking player shoots on goal with a head or performs a pass by a head to another attacking player for shooting on goal with a head or a foot from the limited space. Defending players **passively confront** attacking players **in supporting position**. **Variants:** a) points of players' initial positions inside the limited space and a partner of attacking players are varied; b) defending players actively confronts attacking players **in supporting position**;	– attacking players should try to perform shots on goal or passes with a head for a following shot on goal depending on the trajectory of the ball and actions of defending players and the goalkeeper; – attacking players should shoot on goal and pass with a head also with a physical contact with an opponent; – attacking players should perform shots on goal from any, even inconvenient positions;

Task 3 continuation	
Task description	Requirements for task performance quality

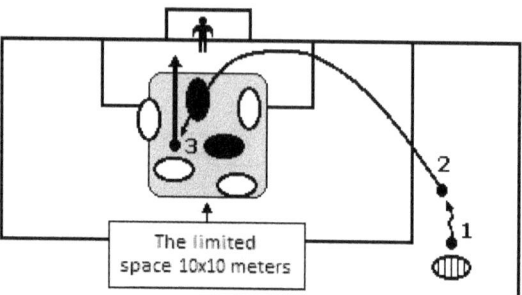

c) in the initial position attacking players are positioned at some distance from the limited space and move into the limited space in different directions after a pass from a partner to shoot on goal	– attacking players should try to send the ball with a head into the area of the goal, unprotected by the goalkeeper, every time

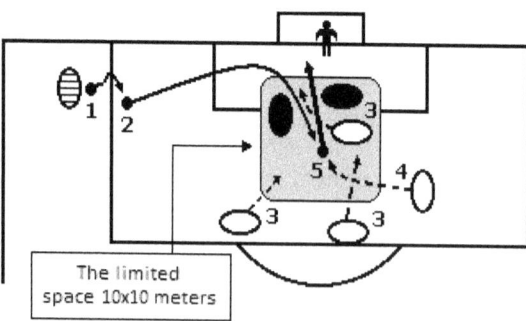

d) defending players **actively confront** attacking players **inside the limited space**

Drills with a variative beginning and variative finishing of players' of actions with the ball

Task 1	
Task description	Requirements for task performance quality
Three on three play with three «neutral» players, acting for the attacking team all the time, two of which act beyond sidelines. Pitch size: 35 meters wide, 25 meters long. Two neutral players act beyond sidelines all the time: one on the right and another on the left. 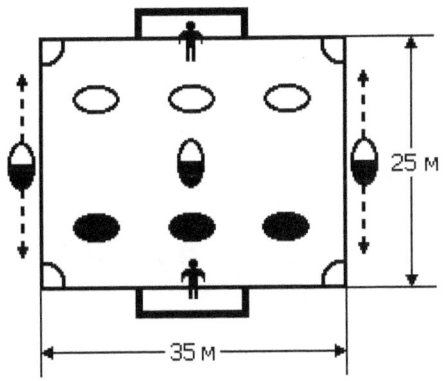 Goalkeepers put the ball into play for players acting on the pitch after catching it or when it crosses the goal-line from players of the attacking team. Players from the attacking team should pass the ball to one on «neutral» players, acting beyond sidelines.	– goalkeepers should put the ball into play without a delay; – having come over the ball, players acting on the pitch should quickly pass it to «neutral» players acting beyond sidelines; – «neutral» players acting beyond sidelines should intentionally send the ball towards the opponents' goal with a mounted trajectory; – players should perform shots on goal and passes with a head from any, even inconvenient positions; – players should try to perform shots on goal and passes with a head also with a physical contact with an opponent;

Task 1 continuation	
Task description	Requirements for task performance quality
Number of passes to each other by attacking players acting on the pitch before sending the ball to a «neutral» player acting beyond the sideline is no more than one. «Neutral» players acting beyond sidelines should send the ball towards the opponents' goal obligingly with a mounted trajectory so that partners could perform a shot on goal with a head or a pass with a head for shooting on goal with a head or a foot. In case the ball crosses the goal-line of the defending team from the goalkeeper and players of this team, «neutral» players acting beyond sidelines, should perform corner kicks, necessarily sending the ball towards the opponents' goal with a mounted trajectory. In case the ball crosses the sideline, «neutral» players acting beyond sidelines should send the ball with a foot towards the opponents' goal necessarily with a mounted trajectory. Players from the defending team try to prevent attacking players to shoot on goal. Players are permitted to finish off the ball into the net. Goal scored at the rebound counts as two. Offsides are not given. Play time in one repeat – 10 minutes. **Variant:** three on three play with two «neutral» players, acting for the attacking team all the time and beyond sidelines	– players should try to use every opportunity to finish off the ball into the net; – while performing shots on goal, players should try to send the ball into the area of the goal, unprotected by the goalkeeper, every time

Task 2	
Task description	Requirements for task performance quality
Six attacking players on two defending players play in two zones, positioned at some distance from each other, providing performing passes from zone to zone with a mounted trajectory. Two zones 10 meters wide and 15 meters long are marked on the pitch 10 meters from each other. Goals are mounted on the opposite short sides of different zones. Three attacking and one defending player act in each zone all the time. Players are prohibited from moving from zone to zone. 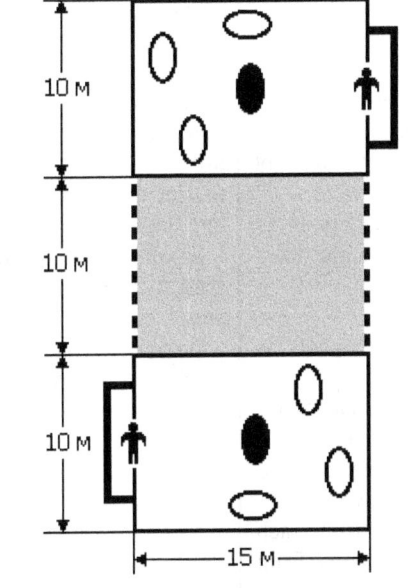	– goalkeepers should put the ball into play without a delay; – defending players should try to intercept the ball or attack an opponent at reception of the ball, entering into physical contact with him; – attacking players, acting in the same zone, should pass the ball to each other timely and precisely, providing the partner with time for performing a pass into the opposite zone; – defending players should attack an opponent, who has gained possession of the ball, as fast as possible, forcing him to act amid time and space shortage; – players should intentionally send the ball into the opposite zone with a mounted trajectory;

Task 2 continuation	
Task description	Requirements for task performance quality
Goalkeepers put the ball into play to the zone where they protect their goal after catching it or when it leaves this area. Three attacking players try to pass the ball into the opposite zone obligingly with a mounted trajectory so that a partner could perform a shot on goal with a head or a pass with a head for shooting on goal with a head or a foot. Number of passes to each other by attacking players who have received the ball from the goalkeeper before sending it to the opposite zone is no more than two. Number of passes to each other by attacking players who have received the ball from the opposite zone before shooting on goal is no more than one. One of defending players tries to prevent attacking players from passing into the opposite zone, while the another – to shoot on goal. The task for six attacking players is to score as much goals as possible in a definite time. Offsides are not given. Goal scored with a first touch counts as two. Goal scored at the rebound counts as two. Play time in one repeat – 10 minutes. **Variant:** four attacking players on two defending players play in two zones, positioned at some distance from each other, providing performing passes from zone to zone with a mounted trajectory	– attacking players, positioned in different zones, should act simultaneously while trying to deliver the ball from zone to zone; – players should perform shots on goal and passes with a head from any, even inconvenient positions; – players should shoot on goal and pass with a head also with a physical contact with an opponent; – players should try to use every opportunity to finish off the ball into the net; – players should try to send the ball into the area of the goal, unprotected by the goalkeeper, every time

Soccer. Training the «game episodes technique», beginning from coming over the ball in open play

Task 3	
Task description	Requirements for task performance quality
Three on three play with a «neutral» player acting for the attacking team all the time with goals positioned diagonally relative to each other. Pitch size: 30 meters wide, 15 meters long. Goals are dislocated relative to each other every which way along the goal-line and mounted 5 meters from pitch corners. 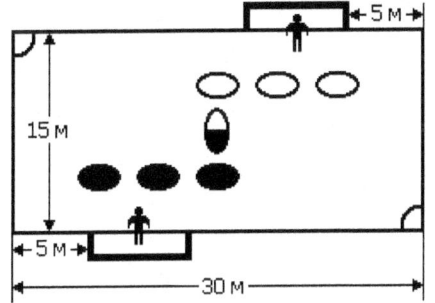 Goalkeepers put the ball into play after catching it or when it crosses the goal-line from players of the attacking team. If the ball leaves the pitch through the sideline players put it into play with hands. Corners are performed from pitch corners distant relative to the goal. Offsides are not given. A goal scored with a head counts as three, while a shot on target with a head – as a goal. Goal scored at the rebound counts as two. Play time in one repeat – 5 minutes	– goalkeepers should put the ball into play without a delay; – players should look for an opportunity to perform a pass with a mounted trajectory for shooting on goal with a head; – players should shoot on goal with a foot or a head from any, even inconvenient positions; – players should try to perform shots on goal and passes with a foot and a head also with a physical contact with an opponent; – players should try to use every opportunity to finish off the ball into the net; – while performing shots on goal with a foot and a head, players should try to send the ball into the area of the goal, unprotected by the goalkeeper, every time

CHAPTER 4.
PERFECTION OF THE «GAME EPISODES TECHNIQUE» IN THE ATTACKING ZONE

Characteristics of the drills construction

Principal task that should be solved while training the «game episodes technique» in the attacking zone is the perfection of the technique of:
– coming over the ball after passes from partners, while tackling and intercepting the ball;
– delivery of the ball into the 18-yard box and scoring from it;
– scoring from the outside of the 18-yard box.

There are several provisions that have to be considered while constructing drills for perfection of the «game episodes technique».

First. Shots on goal from inside and outside of the 18-yard box and the last move (a pass or a movement with the ball) before the shooting should be performed from areas of which goals are scored and the last move before the goalscoring is made in competitive matches.

If it is assumed that a drill would be finished with a shot on goal inside the 18-yard box, then, while performing passes bringing players to the finishing shot in the 18-yard box from area positioned 16 to 35 meters from the goal-line of the defending team, the ball should be sent at an angle (with or without crossing the central lengthwise axis of the pitch) or perpendicularly (or close to this direction) relative to the goal-line depending on the point of coming over the ball across the width of the pitch (fig. 10).

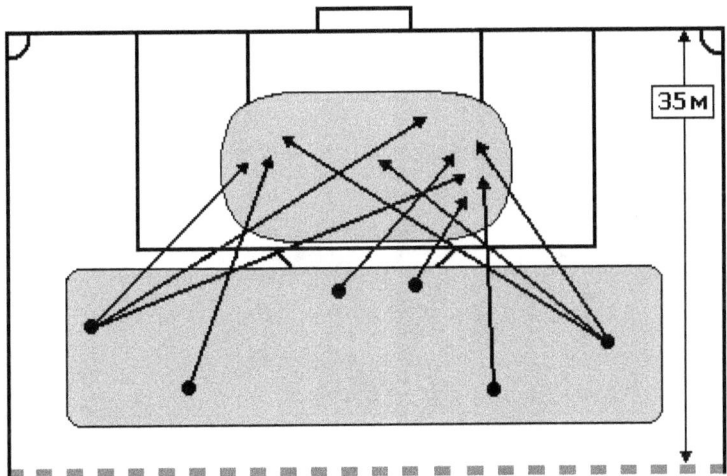

Fig. 10. Directions of passes into the 18-yard box from areas which are 16 to 35 meters from the defending team goal-line, for shooting on goal in drills for perfection of the «game episodes technique» in the attacking zone

In case the ball is delivered into the 18-yard box for shooting on goal from the area which is 16 to 35 meters from the defending team goal-line using dribbling, movements with the ball either with or without beating an opponents should basically be performed in two directions:
– perpendicularly or at some angle to the goal-line through corridors that may be formed by the extension of sidelines of the 18-yard box and the goal area into the areas to the left and to the right nearly between angles of the goal area and 18-yard box;
– perpendicularly or at some angle to the goal-line in a corridor approx. 15 meters wide opposite to the goal into the area which is between the 18-yard box line and the penalty spot (fig. 11).

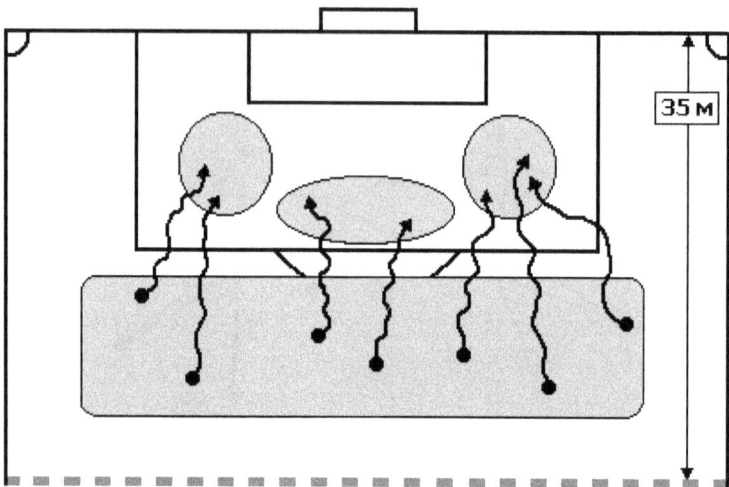

Fig. 11. Directions of movements with the ball into the 18-yard box from areas which are 16 to 35 meters from the defending team goal-line, for shooting on goal in drills for perfection of the «game episodes technique» in the attacking zone

While performing passes bringing to the finishing shot in the 18-yard box from areas between pitch and 18-yard box sidelines, the ball should be sent in parallel to the goal-line or close to this direction basically into the area opposite to the goal between the penalty spot and the goal-area line (fig. 12).

It is appropriate to perform movements with the ball from areas positioned between sidelines of the pitch and of the 18-yard box into the 18-yard box with or without outplaying an opponent and a following shot on goal in parallel or at some angle to the goal-line away from the goal into areas between corners of the goal-area and the 18-yard box (fig. 13).

Soccer. Training the «game episodes technique», beginning from coming over the ball in open play

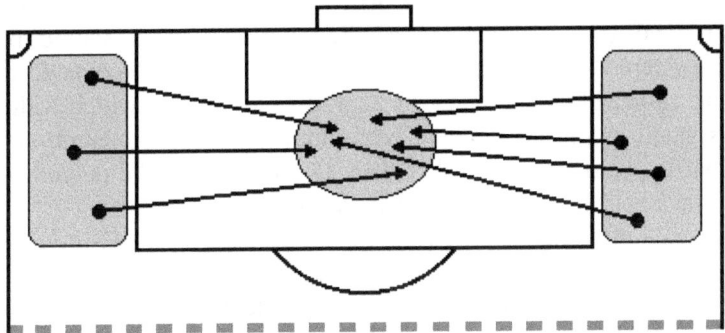

Fig. 12. Directions of passes into the 18-yard box from areas between sidelines of the pitch and of the 18-yard box for shooting on goal in drills for perfection of the «game episodes technique» in the attacking zone

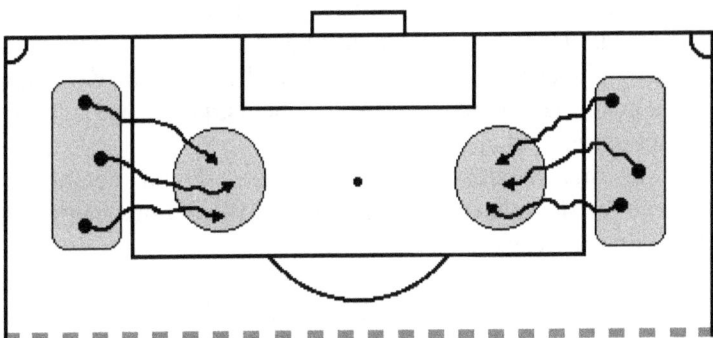

Fig. 13. Directions of movements with the ball into the 18-yard box from areas between sidelines of the pitch and of the 18-yard box for shooting on goal in drills for perfection of the «game episodes technique» in the attacking zone

If it is supposed that a drill would be finished with a shot on goal from the outside of the 18-yard box, it should be considered that in competitive matches goal from the outside of the 18-yard box are generally scored from the area which width is smaller than the 18-yard box width (approx. 30 meters) and that is positioned no further than 25 meters from the defending team's goal-line, in following situations:

– after movements with the ball at short distance;

– after passes on short and medium distances in parallel to the goal-line and away from the opponents' 18-yard box line towards the attacking team's goal.

Second. Drills in which players should perform several actions (deliver the ball into the 18-yard box or in certain areas beyond it, and then perform the last move before shooting on goal) after coming over the ball and before shooting on goal) should contain no more than three such actions, while time of the attack should be no more than 10 seconds.

Third. One of characteristics of attacks in the zone no further than 35 meters from the opponents' goal-line is that an attacking player with the ball, positioned face to the defending team's goal, may be attacked by opponents, positioned not only in front of him, but also behind.

In this regards attacking players should notably be required for **the maximum quickness of the actions beginning after coming over the ball.**

Fourth. While performing gaming drills, attacking actions after coming over the ball as a result of a tackle or an interception should begin at the same distance from the goal-line as the one at which goalscoring attack generally begin after a tackle or an interception in competitive matches – 20 to 35 meters to the defending team's goal-line.

Following are examples of drills for perfection of the «game episodes technique» in the attacking zone.

Drills in which the ball is delivered into the 18-yard box by means of dribbling

Task 1	
Task description	Requirements for task performance quality
Players' initial position, sequence of their actions and directions of movement	

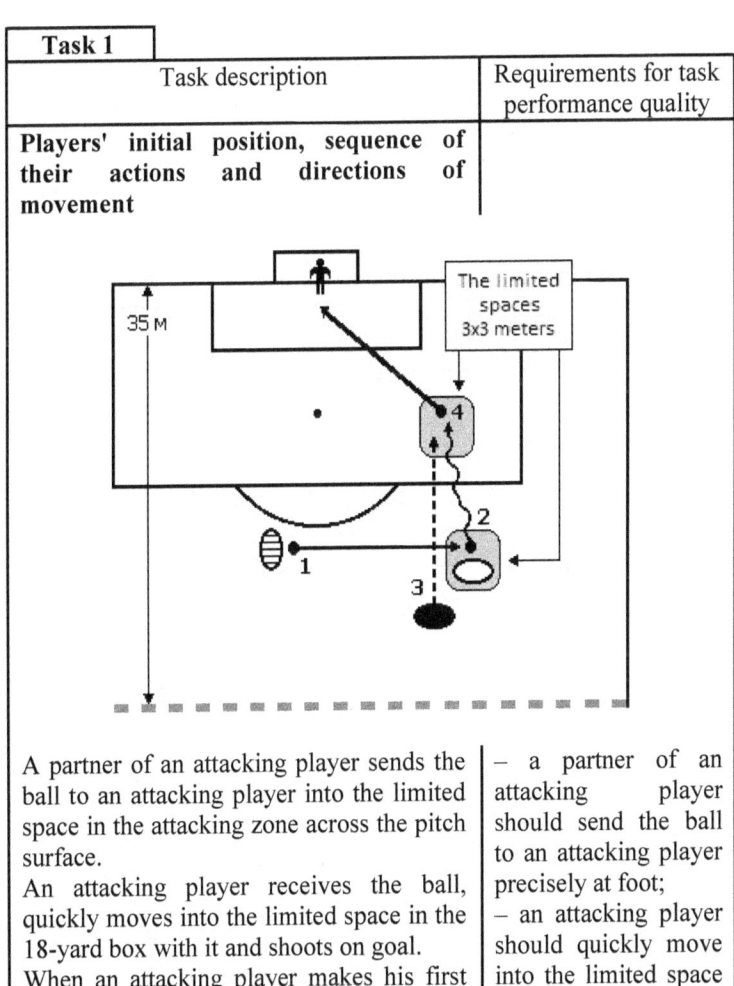

A partner of an attacking player sends the ball to an attacking player into the limited space in the attacking zone across the pitch surface. An attacking player receives the ball, quickly moves into the limited space in the 18-yard box with it and shoots on goal. When an attacking player makes his first touch of the ball, a defending player begins to move towards an attacking player and tries to prevent him from shooting on goal from the limited space in the 18-yard box.	– a partner of an attacking player should send the ball to an attacking player precisely at foot; – an attacking player should quickly move into the limited space with the ball and shoot on goal;

Task 1 continuation	
Task description	Requirements for task performance quality
Variants: a) points of marking of limited spaces and players' initial position are varied; b) in initial position an attacking player is positioned at some distance from the limited space in the attacking zone and moves into it in different directions to receive the ball.	– an attacking player should shoot on goal also with a physical contact with a defending player; – an attacking player should shoot on goal from the limited space exactly;

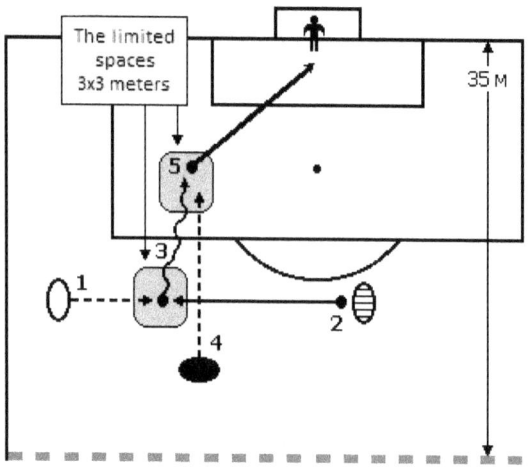

Note. A distance at which a defending player is positioned in the initial position from an attacking space should be such that he could be close enough to an attacking player, beginning the movement when the latter touches the ball, but at the same time that an attacking player could shoot on goal from the limited space inside the 18-yard box, acting with a maximum speed and precision	– an attacking player should try to send the ball into the area of the goal, unprotected by the goalkeeper, every time

Soccer. Training the «game episodes technique», beginning from coming over the ball in open play

Task 2		
	Task description	Requirements for task performance quality
	Players' initial position, sequence of their actions and directions of movement	– a defending player should send the ball to an attacking player precisely at foot;
	[Diagram: field layout showing 35 M distance, "The limited space 4x4 meters" with players B, 5, 3, A, 4, 5 arranged, and "The limited space 3x3 meters" with players 3, 1, 2]	
	A defending player, positioned in the attacking zone, sends the ball to an attacking player, positioned in the attacking zone, across the pitch surface. An attacking player receives the ball, quickly moves with it into the limited space at the corner of the 18-yard box and shoots on goal (variant A) or performs a pass to a partner into the limited space opposite to the goal for shooting on goal (variant B). A defending player positioned in the attacking zone begins to move into the limited space opposite to the goal when an attacking player makes his first touch of the ball and tries to prevent a partner of an attacking player to shoot on goal.	– an attacking player should quickly move into the limited space with the ball and shoot on goal or perform a pass to a partner; – an attacking player should pass to a partner most accurately; – attacking players should shoot on goal from limited spaces exactly;

Task 2 continuation	
Task description	Requirements for task performance quality
A defending player positioned in the limited space opposite to the goal begins to move into the limited space opposite to the goal when an attacking player makes his first touch of the ball and tries to prevent an attacking player to deliver the ball into this limited space and shoot on goal or perform a pass to a partner from it. **Variants:** a) a defending player sends the ball to an attacking player with a bounce off the pitch surface and on air low-level; b) points of marking of limited spaces and players' initial position are varied; 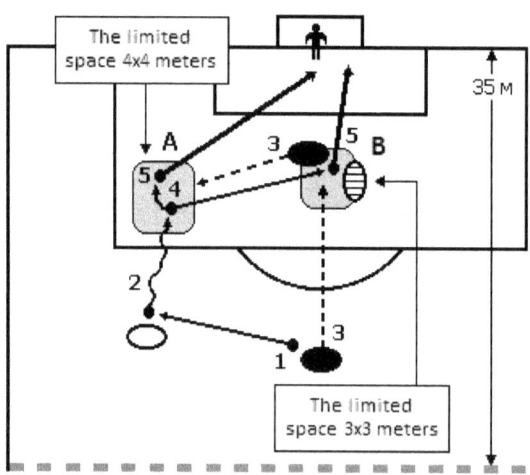 c) in initial position an attacking player moves in various directions in the attacking zone for receiving the ball.	– attacking players should shoot on goal also with a physical contact with a defending player; – attacking players should try to send the ball into the area of the goal, unprotected by the goalkeeper, every time

Task 2 continuation	
Task description	Requirements for task performance quality
Notes. 1. A distance at which a defending player is positioned in initial position in the attacking zone from the limited space opposite to the goal should be such that he could come up with a partner of an attacking player when the latter shoots on goal, beginning the movement when an attacking player makes his first touch of the ball, but at the same time that a partner of an attacking player could shoot on goal providing that an attacking player delivers the ball into the limited space at the corner of the 18-yard box with a maximum speed and performs an accurate pass to him into the limited space opposite to the goal. 2. A distance between limited spaces should be such that a defending player, positioned in the limited space opposite to the goal, could come up with an attacking player when the latter shoots on goal or performing a pass to a partner, beginning a movement when an attacking player makes his first touch of the ball, but at the same time that an attacking player could shoot on goal or perform a pass to a partner from the limited space at the 18-yard box corner, acting with a maximum speed and precision	

Task 3	
Task description	Requirements for task performance quality
Players' initial position, sequence of their actions and directions of movement	– a defending player should send the ball to attacking players precisely at foot;
[Diagram: A field area 35 m showing "The limited spaces 10x5 meters", with positions A, B, and numbered players 1, 2, 3, 4, 5 with arrows indicating movement directions]	
A defending player, positioned in the attacking zone, sends the ball to one of attacking players into the limited space in the attacking zone across the pitch surface. An attacking player receives the ball, quickly moves with it into the limited space in the 18-yard box and shoots on goal (variant A) or performs a pass to a partner into the limited space for shooting on goal with a first or a second touch (variant B). A defending player, positioned in the limited space in the attacking zone, tries to prevent attacking players from delivering the ball into the limited space in the 18-yard box and shooting on goal.	– attacking players should quickly move into the limited space in the 18-yard box with the ball and shoot on goal; – an attacking player should pass to a partner most accurately; – attacking players should shoot on goal from the limited space exactly;

Soccer. Training the «game episodes technique», beginning from coming over the ball in open play

Task 3 continuation	
Task description	Requirements for task performance quality
A defending player positioned in the attacking zone begins to move into the 18-yard box when an attacking player makes his first touch of the ball and tries to prevent attacking players from shooting on goal. **Variant:** points of marking of limited spaces and players' initial position are varied.	– attacking players should shoot on goal also with a physical contact with a defending player; – attacking players should try to send the ball into the area of the goal, unprotected by the goalkeeper, every time

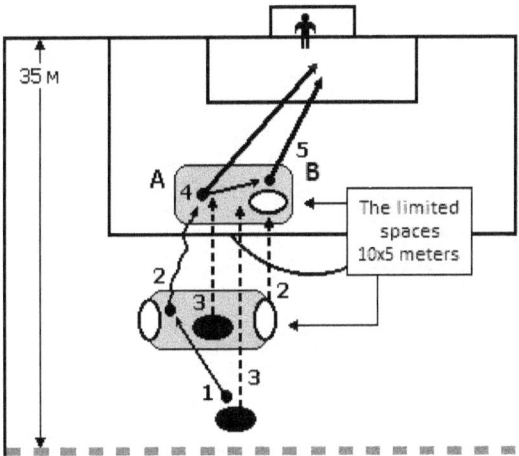

Note. A distance at which a defending player is positioned in the initial position in the attacking zone from attacking players should be such that he could come up with attacking players when they shoot on goal, beginning the movement when an attacking player makes his first touch of the ball, but at the same time that attacking players could shoot on goal, acting with a maximum speed and precision

Task 4	
Task description	Requirements for task performance quality
Players' initial position, sequence of their actions and directions of movement An attacking player is positioned in the limited space in the attacking zone back to the opponent's goal. 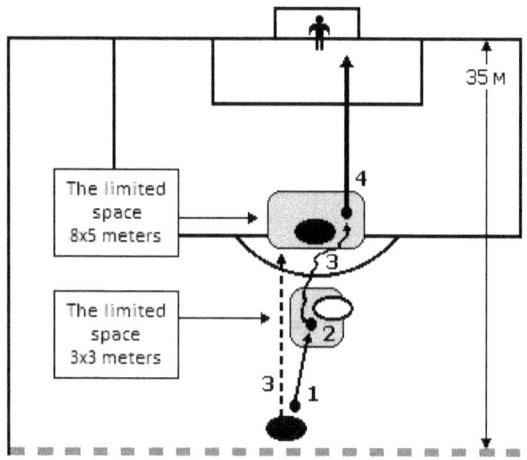 A defending player, positioned in the attacking zone, sends the ball to an attacking player into the limited space in the attacking zone across the pitch surface. An attacking player receives the ball with a twist, quickly moves into the limited space in the 18-yard box with it, beats a defending player and shoots on goal from the limited space. A defending player positioned in the attacking zone begins to move into the 18-yard box when an attacking player makes his first touch of the ball and tries to prevent an attacking player from shooting on goal.	– a defending player should send the ball to an attacking player precisely at foot; – an attacking player should quickly perform a twist with the ball, move into the limited space with the ball, beat an opponent and shoot on goal; – an attacking player should shoot on goal from the limited space exactly;

Soccer. Training the «game episodes technique», beginning from coming over the ball in open play

Task 4 continuation	
Task description	Requirements for task performance quality
Variants: a) points of marking of limited spaces and players' initial position are varied; b) in initial position an attacking player is positioned at some distance from the limited space in the attacking zone and moves into it in different directions to receive the ball back to the opponents' goal.	– an attacking player should shoot on goal also with a physical contact with a defending player; – an attacking player should try to send the ball into the area of the goal, unprotected by the goalkeeper, every time
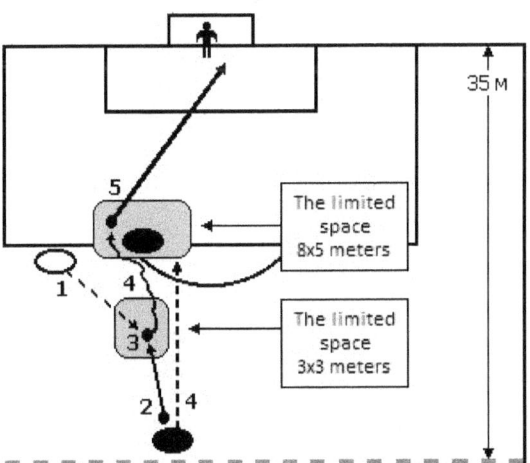	
Note. A distance at which a defending player is positioned in the initial position from an attacking player in the attacking zone should be such that he could be close enough to an attacking player, beginning the movement when the latter touches the ball, but at the same time that an attacking player could shoot on goal, acting with a maximum speed and precision	

Task 5

Task description	Requirements for task performance quality
Players' initial position, sequence of their actions and directions of movement An attacking player is positioned in the limited space back to the goal.	– a defending player should send the ball to an attacking player precisely at foot;

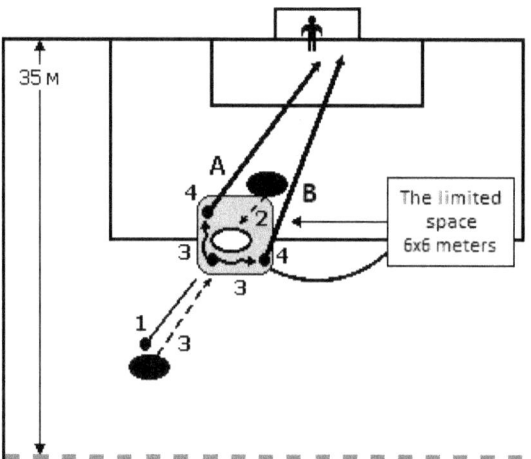

A defending player, positioned in the attacking zone, sends the ball to an attacking player into the limited space across the pitch surface. An attacking player receives the ball back to the opponents' goal, beats a defending player to the right in the limited space while moving into the 18-yard box or to the left while moving along the 18-yard box line, and shoots on goal from the limited space from the 18-yard box (variant A) or from beyond it (variant B).	– an attacking player should quickly twist with the ball, beat an opponent and shoot on goal; – an attacking player should shoot on goal from the limited space exactly; – an attacking player should shoot on goal also with a physical contact with a defending player;

Task 5 continuation	
Task description	Requirements for task performance quality
After a pass from a defending player positioned in the attacking zone, a defending player positioned at the limited space in the 18-yard box, begins to move into the limited space and tries to prevent an attacking player from shooting on goal. A defending player positioned in the attacking zone begins to move into the limited space when an attacking player makes his first touch of the ball and tries to prevent an attacking player from shooting on goal. **Variants:** a) points of marking of the limited space on the 18-yard box line and players' initial position are varied; b) in initial position an attacking player is positioned at some distance from the limited space and moves into it in different directions to receive the ball back to the opponents' goal. **Note.** A distance at which a defending player is positioned in the initial position in the attacking zone from an attacking player should be such that he could come up with an attacking player when he shoots on goal, beginning the movement when an attacking player makes his first touch of the ball, but at the same time that an attacking player could shoot on goal, acting with a maximum speed and precision	– an attacking player should try to send the ball into the area of the goal, unprotected by the goalkeeper, every time

Task 6	
Task description	Requirements for task performance quality
Players' initial position, sequence of their actions and directions of movement	– a defending player should send the ball to an attacking player precisely at foot;

(Diagram: field area showing 35 м distance, a limited space 3x3 meters and a limited space 6x6 meters, with players numbered 1, 2, 3, 4)

A defending player, positioned in the attacking zone, sends the ball to an attacking player into the limited space in the attacking zone across the pitch surface. An attacking player receives the ball, quickly moves into the limited space in the 18-yard box with it, beats a defending player and shoots on goal. A defending player positioned in the attacking zone begins to move into the 18-yard box when an attacking player makes his first touch of the ball and tries to prevent an attacking player from shooting on goal. **Variants:** a) points of marking of the limited space and players' initial position are varied;	– an attacking player should quickly move into the limited space in the 18-yard box, beat an opponent and shoot on goal; – an attacking player should shoot on goal from the limited space exactly; – an attacking player should shoot on goal also with a physical contact with a defending player;

Task 6 continuation	
Task description	Requirements for task performance quality
b) in initial position an attacking player is positioned at some distance from the limited space in the attacking zone and moves into it in different directions to receive the ball.	– an attacking player should try to send the ball into the area of the goal, unprotected by the goalkeeper, every time

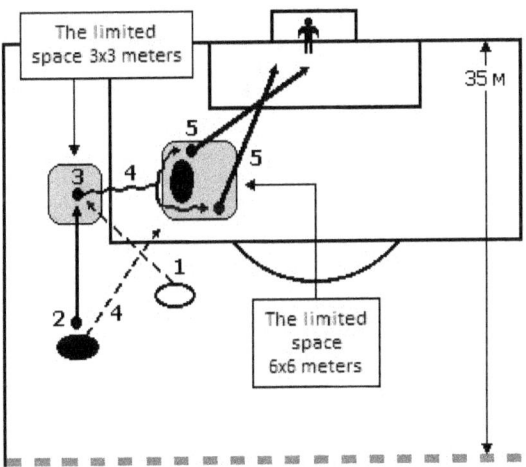

Notes. 1. A distance between limited spaces may vary from 5 to 12 meters. 2. A distance at which a defending player is positioned in the initial position in the attacking zone from an attacking player should be such that he could come up with an attacking player when he shoots on goal, beginning the movement when an attacking player makes his first touch of the ball, but at the same time that an attacking player could shoot on goal, acting with a maximum speed and precision	

Task 7	
Task description	Requirements for task performance quality
Players' initial position, sequence of their actions and directions of movement	– a defending player should send the ball to an attacking player precisely at foot;

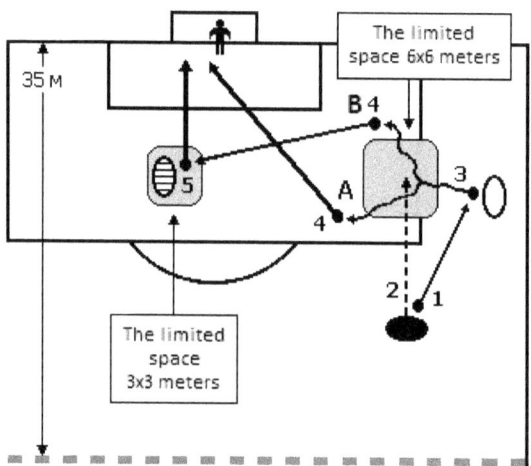

A defending player sends the ball to an attacking player, positioned in the attacking zone, across the pitch surface and begins to move into the limited space at the 18-yard box sideline. An attacking player receives the ball, quickly moves with it into the limited space at the 18-yard box sideline, beats a defending player to the left or to the right side and shoots on goal from the 18-yard box (variant A) or performs a pass to a partner into the limited space opposite to the goal for shooting on goal **with a first touch** (variant B). A defending player tries to prevent an attacking player to:	– an attacking player should quickly move into the 18-yard box, beat an opponent and shoot on goal or perform a pass to a partner; – an attacking player should shoot on goal also with a physical contact with a defending player; – a partner of an attacking player should shoot on goal with a first touch obligingly;

Task 7 continuation	
Task description	Requirements for task performance quality
a) deliver the ball into the 18-yard box through the limited space; b) perform a shot on goal or a pass to a partner from the 18-yard box. **Variants:** a) points of marking of limited spaces and players' initial position are varied; b) a defending player sends the ball to an attacking player, moving in various directions in the area between pitch and 18-yard box sidelines for receiving the ball.	– attacking players should try to send the ball into the area of the goal, unprotected by the goalkeeper, every time

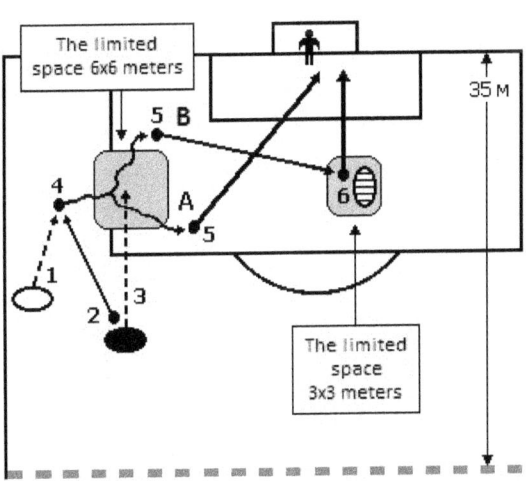

| Note. A distance at which a defending player is positioned in the initial position from the limited space at the 18-yard box sideline should be such that he could get into the limited space a bit earlier than an attacking player or at the same time with him, beginning his movement after a pass | |

Drills in which the ball is delivered into the 18-yard box by means of a pass

Task 1	
Task description	Requirements for task performance quality
Players' initial position, sequence of their actions and directions of movement	– a defending player should send the ball to an attacking player precisely at foot;

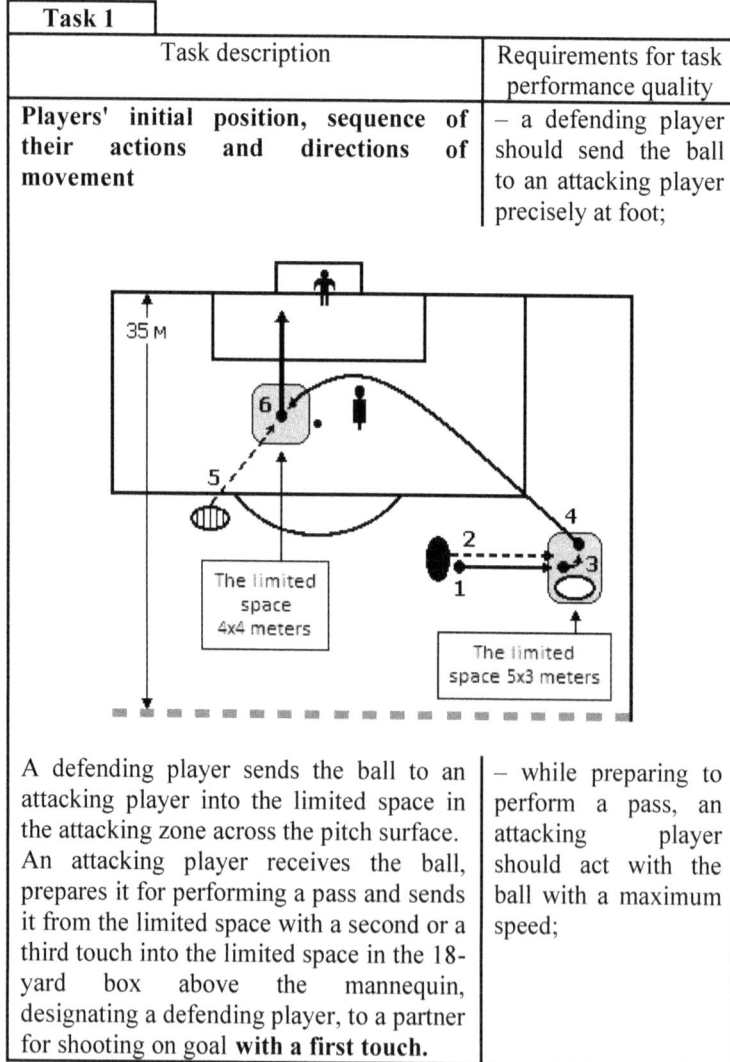

A defending player sends the ball to an attacking player into the limited space in the attacking zone across the pitch surface. An attacking player receives the ball, prepares it for performing a pass and sends it from the limited space with a second or a third touch into the limited space in the 18-yard box above the mannequin, designating a defending player, to a partner for shooting on goal **with a first touch.**	– while preparing to perform a pass, an attacking player should act with the ball with a maximum speed;

Task 1 continuation	
Task description	Requirements for task performance quality
Having performed a pass, a defending player begins to move into the limited space in the attacking zone and tries to prevent an attacking players from performing a pass. A partner of an attacking player moves into the limited space in the 18-yard box and shoots on goal with a first touch of a foot or a head obligingly. **Variants:** a) a defending player sends the ball to an attacking player with a bounce off the pitch surface and on air low-level; b) points of marking of limited spaces and players' initial position are varied; c) in initial position an attacking player is positioned at some distance from the limited space in the attacking zone and moves into it in different directions to receive the ball; d) a partner of an attacking player moves into the limited space with change of direction of movement. **Note.** A distance at which a defending player is positioned in the initial position from the limited space in the attacking zone should be such that he could come up with an attacking player when the latter performs a pass, beginning the movement after performing a pass, but at the same time that an attacking player could perform a pass, acting with a maximum speed and precision	– an attacking player should send the ball to his partner precisely into the limited space with the lowest possible trajectory, yet so that it flew above a mannequin designating a defending player; – a partner of an attacking player should begin to move into the 18-yard box timely relative to the moment of the pass performing by an attacking player; – a partner of an attacking player should shoot on goal with a first touch obligingly; – a partner of an attacking player should try to send the ball into the area of the goal, unprotected by the goalkeeper, every time

Task 2	
Task description	Requirements for task performance quality
Players' initial position, sequence of their actions and directions of movement	– a defending player should send the ball to an attacking player precisely at foot;
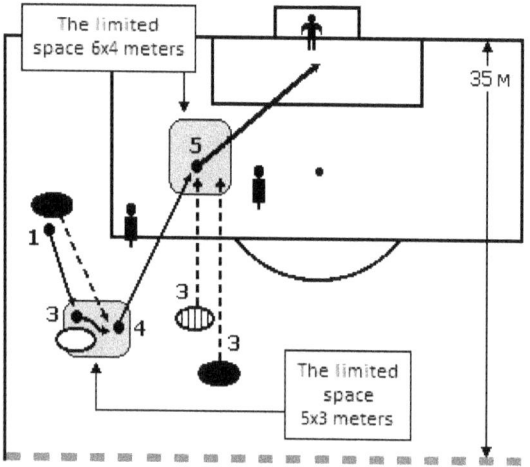	
A defending player, positioned at the corner of the 18-yard box, sends the ball to an attacking player into the limited space in the attacking zone across the pitch surface. An attacking player receives the ball, prepares it for performing a pass and sends it from the limited space into the limited space in the 18-yard box across the pitch surface to a partner for shooting on goal **with a first or a second touch.** Having performed a pass, a defending player, positioned at the corner of the 18-yard box, begins to move into the limited space in the attacking zone and tries to prevent an attacking players from performing a pass.	– while preparing to perform a pass, an attacking player should act with the ball with a maximum speed; – a defending player should send the ball into the limited space precisely and with a necessary speed;

Soccer. Training the «game episodes technique», beginning from coming over the ball in open play

Task 2 continuation	
Task description	Requirements for task performance quality
A partner of an attacking player moves into the limited space in the 18-yard box and shoots on goal with a first or a second touch obligingly. A defending player, positioned behind the back of a partner of an attacking player, begins to move into the 18-yard box simultaneously with him and tries to prevent him from shooting on goal. **Variants:** a) a defending player sends the ball to an attacking player with a bounce off the pitch surface and on air low-level; b) points of marking of limited spaces and players' initial position are varied; c) in initial position an attacking player is positioned at some distance from the limited space in the attacking zone and moves into it in different directions to receive the ball. **Notes.** 1. A distance at which a defending player is positioned in the initial position at the corner of the 18-yard box from an attacking player should be such that he could come up with an attacking player when the latter performs a pass, beginning the movement after performing a pass, but at the same time that an attacking player could perform a pass, acting with a maximum speed and precision. 2. A distance between a partner of an attacking player and a defending player behind his back is 4-5 meters	– a partner of an attacking player should begin to move into the 18-yard box timely relative to the moment of the pass performing by an attacking player; – a partner of an attacking player should come over the ball and shoot on goal without reducing the speed of movement; – a partner of an attacking player should shoot on goal with a first or second touch obligingly; – a partner of an attacking player should try to send the ball into the area of the goal, unprotected by the goalkeeper, every time

Task 3

Task description	Requirements for task performance quality
Players' initial position, sequence of their actions and directions of movement	– a defending player should send the ball to an attacking player precisely at foot;

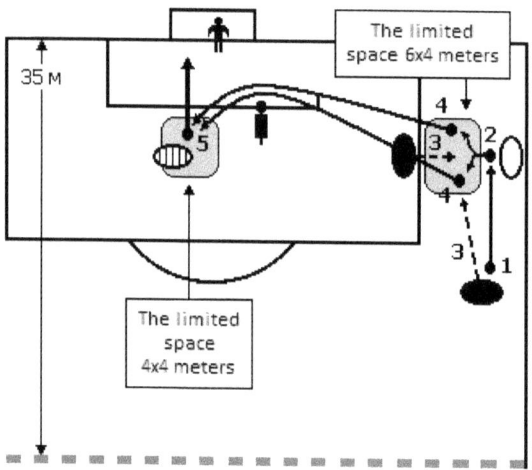

A defending player, positioned in the attacking zone, sends the ball to an attacking player across the pitch surface. An attacking player receives the ball, beats a defending player in the limited space in the attacking zone to the left or to the right and sends the ball to a partner into the limited space in the 18-yard box above a mannequin designating a defending player for shooting on goal **with a first touch of a foot or a head.** Having performed a pass, a defending player, positioned at the 18-yard box sideline, begins to move into the limited space in the attacking zone when an	– an attacking player should quickly beat an opponent and perform a pass to a partner; – an attacking player should send the ball to his partner precisely into the limited space with the lowest possible trajectory, yet so that it flew above a mannequin designating a defending player;

Soccer. Training the «game episodes technique», beginning from coming over the ball in open play

Task 3 continuation	
Task description	Requirements for task performance quality
attacking player firstly touches the ball and tries to prevent an attacking players from performing a pass. A defending player, positioned in the attacking zone, begins to move into the limited space in the attacking zone when an attacking player firstly touches the ball and tries to prevent an attacking players from performing a pass. **Variants:** a) a defending player sends the ball to an attacking player with a bounce off the pitch surface and on air low-level; b) points of marking of limited spaces and players' initial position are varied; c) in initial position an attacking player is positioned at some distance from the limited space in the attacking zone and moves into it in different directions to receive the ball; d) in initial position a partner of an attacking player is positioned at some distance from the limited space in the 18-yard box and moves into it in different directions to shoot on goal. **Note.** A distance at which a defending player is positioned in the initial position in the attacking zone from an attacking player should be such that he could come up with an attacking player when he performs a pass, beginning the movement when an attacking player makes his first touch of the ball, but at the same time that an attacking player could perform a pass, acting with a maximum speed and precision	– a defending player, positioned at the 18-yard box sideline, should try to prevent an attacking player from performing a pass for a longest possible time for the second defending player to get in time to move into the limited space in the attacking zone; – a partner of an attacking player should shoot on goal with a first touch obligingly; – a partner of an attacking player should try to send the ball into the area of the goal, unprotected by the goalkeeper, every time

Task 4

Task description	Requirements for task performance quality
Players' initial position, sequence of their actions and directions of movement	– a defending player should send the ball to an attacking player precisely at foot;

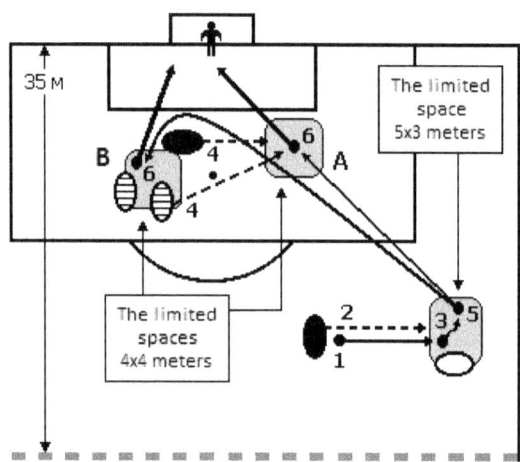

A defending player, positioned in the attacking zone, sends the ball to an attacking player into the limited space in the attacking zone across the pitch surface. An attacking player receives the ball, prepares it for performing a pass and sends it from the limited space to one of his partner into the limited space closer to the goal-line across the pitch surface (variant A) for shooting on goal with a foot or into the limited space distant from the goal-line with a mounted trajectory (variant B) for shooting on goal with a foot or a head. One of partners of an attacking player moves into the limited space closer to the goal-line for receiving the ball and performing a shot on goal.	– while preparing to perform a pass, an attacking player should act with the ball with a maximum speed; – a defending player should send the ball into the limited space precisely and with a necessary speed; – a defending player positioned in the 18-yard box should be positioned at the limited space, distant to the goal-line, in the initial position;

Soccer. Training the «game episodes technique», beginning from coming over the ball in open play

Task 4 continuation	
Task description	Requirements for task performance quality
Having performed a pass, a defending player, positioned in the attacking zone, begins to move into the limited space in the attacking zone and tries to prevent an attacking players from performing a pass. A defending player, positioned in the 18-yard box at the limited space, distant to the goal-line, tries to prevent partners of an attacking player to shoot on goal while moving into the limited space closer to the goal-line or into the limited space distant to the goal-line. **Variants:** a) a defending player sends the ball to an attacking player with a bounce off the pitch surface and on air low-level; b) points of marking of limited spaces and players' initial position are varied; c) in initial position an attacking player is positioned at some distance from the limited space in the attacking zone and moves into it in different directions to receive the ball. **Note.** A distance at which a defending player is positioned in the initial position in the attacking zone from an attacking player should be such that he could come up with an attacking player when the latter performs a pass, beginning the movement after performing a pass, but at the same time that an attacking player could perform a pass, acting with a maximum speed and precision	– a partner of an attacking player should begin moving into the limited space, closer to the goal-line, timely relative to the moment of a pass performance; – partners of an attacking players should shoot on goal from limited spaces exactly; – partners of an attacking player should try to send the ball into the area of the goal, unprotected by the goalkeeper, every time

Task 5	
Task description	Requirements for task performance quality
Players' initial position, sequence of their actions and directions of movement	

Diagram: field layout showing 35 m distance, a limited space 10x4 meters in the attacking zone with players 5, B, 2, A, and another limited space 8x5 meters with players 3, 4; player 1 near goal with goalkeeper.

The goalkeeper sends the ball to an attacking player into the limited space in the attacking zone with a mounted trajectory. An attacking player receives the ball and sends it from the limited space to one of his partners into the limited space in the 18-yard box for shooting on goal **with a first of a second touch**. When an attacking player firstly touches the ball, one of defending players begins to move into the limited space in the attacking zone and tries to prevent an attacking player from performing a pass, while a second one stays in the 18-yard box and tries to prevent partners of an attacking player to shoot on goal.	– the goalkeeper should send the ball to an attacking player precisely in the limited space; – a defending player should attack an attacking player as soon as possible, forcing him to pass the ball amid time shortage for preparing and performing a pass; – an attacking player should send the ball to his partners precisely at foot;

Task 5 continuation	
Task description	Requirements for task performance quality
Variants: a) points of marking of limited spaces and players' initial position are varied; b) in initial position an attacking player is positioned at some distance from the limited space in the attacking zone and moves into it in different directions to receive the ball.	– while preparing to perform a pass, an attacking player should act with the ball with a maximum speed;
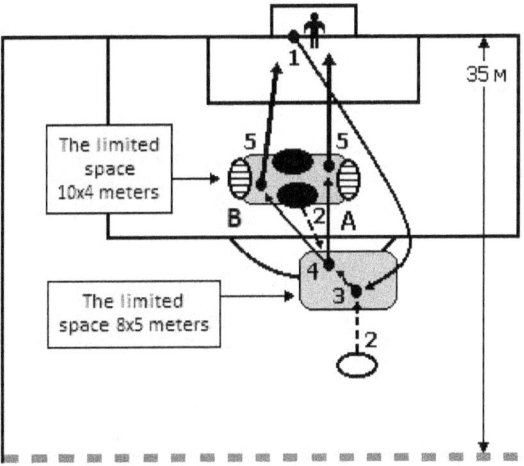	
Notes. 1. A distance between limited spaces varies from 5 to 10 meters. 2. A defending player, moving into the limited space in the attacking zone after a pass from the goalkeeper should be positioned as close to this space as possible in the initial position to come up with an attacking player when the latter performs a pass	– partners of an attacking players should shoot on goal from the limited space exactly; – partners of an attacking player should try to send the ball into the area of the goal, unprotected by the goalkeeper, every time

Task 6	
Task description	Requirements for task performance quality
Four on four play with two «neutral» players acting for the attacking team all the time providing two player acting all the time in the defensive zone, two in attacking zone, one «neutral» in the defensive zone and another – in the attacking zone. Pitch size: 15 meters wide, 35 meters long. Three zones are marked on the pitch: attacking and defensive 14 meters long each and the middle 5 meters long. In each team two players act in their team defensive zone, and two – in the attacking zone all the time. One «neutral» player acting in the defensive area, and another – in the attacking zone all the time. Players are prohibited from moving from zone to zone. Goalkeepers put the ball into play to their team defensive zone after catching it or when it crosses the goal-line and sidelines. Two players from the attacking team and a «neutral» player acting in the defensive zone try to outplay two players from the defending team and pass the ball to their partners in the attacking zone. Two players from the attacking team and a «neutral» player acting in the attacking zone try to outplay two players from the defending team and shoot on goal. Number of passes by attacking players during the attack is no more than three in the defensive zone and no more than two in the attacking zone. Corners are not awarded. Offsides are not given.	– goalkeepers should put the ball into play without a delay into their team's defensive zone obligingly; – players from the attacking team should try to deliver the ball into the attacking zone quickly and shoot on goal; – players from the attacking team should timely open to receive the ball while performing passes from the defensive into the attacking zone; – defending players should attack an opponent, who has gained possession of the ball, as fast as possible, forcing him to act amid time and space shortage; – players should operate with the ball quickly; – players should try shoot on goal also with a first touch; – players should try to use every opportunity to finish off the ball into the net;

Task 6 continuation	
Task description	Requirements for task performance quality
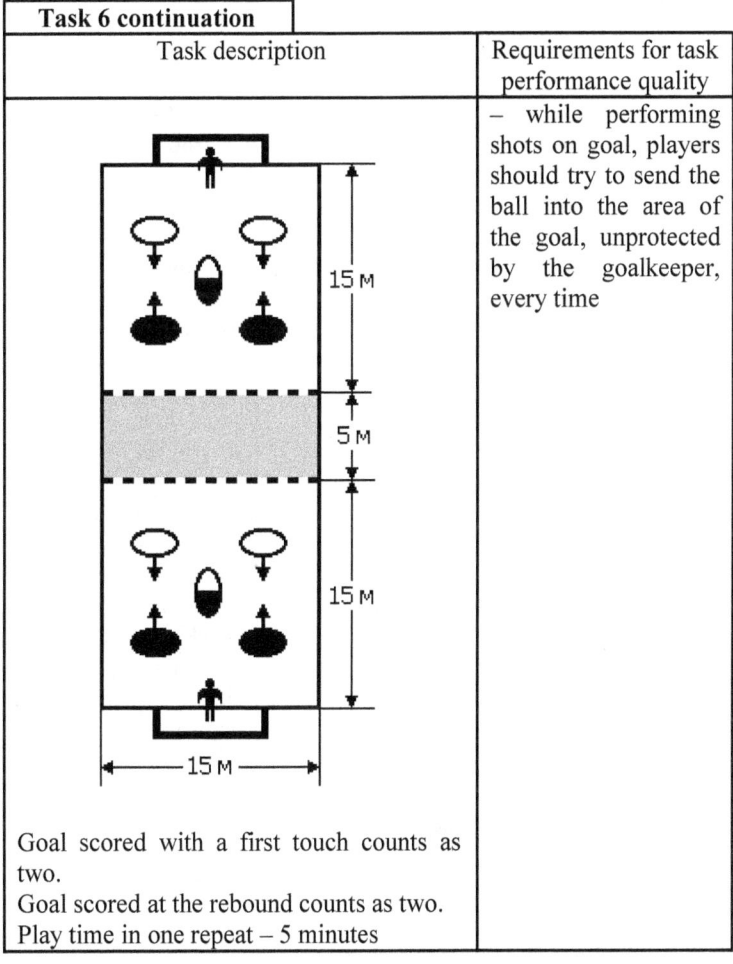 Goal scored with a first touch counts as two. Goal scored at the rebound counts as two. Play time in one repeat – 5 minutes	– while performing shots on goal, players should try to send the ball into the area of the goal, unprotected by the goalkeeper, every time

Task 7	
Task description	Requirements for task performance quality
Four on four play with a «neutral» player acting for the attacking team all the time providing crossing the half-way line by a pass and performing shots on goal from the attacking zone. Pitch size: 20 meters wide, 33 meters long. The half-way line, dividing the pitch in attacking and defensive zones, is marked. 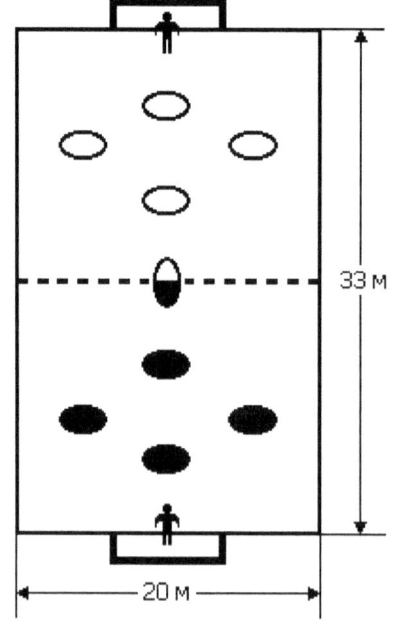 Goalkeepers put the ball into play to their team defensive zone after catching it or when it crosses the goal-line. If the ball leaves the pitch through the sideline players put it into play with hands.	– goalkeepers should put the ball into play without a delay into their team's defensive zone obligingly; – players from the attacking team should try to deliver the ball into the attacking zone quickly and shoot on goal; – players from the attacking team should timely open to receive the ball while performing passes from the defensive into the attacking zone; – defending players should attack an opponent, who has gained possession of the ball, as fast as possible, forcing him to act amid time and space shortage; – players should operate with the ball quickly; – players should try to use every opportunity to finish off the ball into the net;

Soccer. Training the «game episodes technique», beginning from coming over the ball in open play

Task 7 continuation	
Task description	Requirements for task performance quality
Players from the attacking team try to deliver the ball from the defensive into the attacking zone by means of **a pass** and to shoot on goal from this zone. Number of passes by attacking players during the attack is no more than three in the defensive zone and no more than two in the attacking zone. Number of touches of the ball by each player is no more than two in the defensive zone and not restricted in the attacking zone. Players from the defending team try to prevent players from the attacking team from delivering the ball into the attacking zone and shoot on goal while positioning **obligingly in the opponents' defensive zone** when their goalkeeper puts the ball into play. Corners are not awarded. **Offsides are given.** Goal scored with a first touch counts as two. Goal scored at the rebound counts as two. Play time in one repeat – 5 minutes. **Variant:** goals are dislocated relative to each other every which way along the goal-line	– while performing shots on goal, players should try to send the ball into the area of the goal, unprotected by the goalkeeper, every time

Drills in which the ball is delivered into the 18-yard box by means of combination of dribbling and passes

Task 1		
	Task description	Requirements for task performance quality
	Players' initial position, sequence of their actions and directions of movement	
	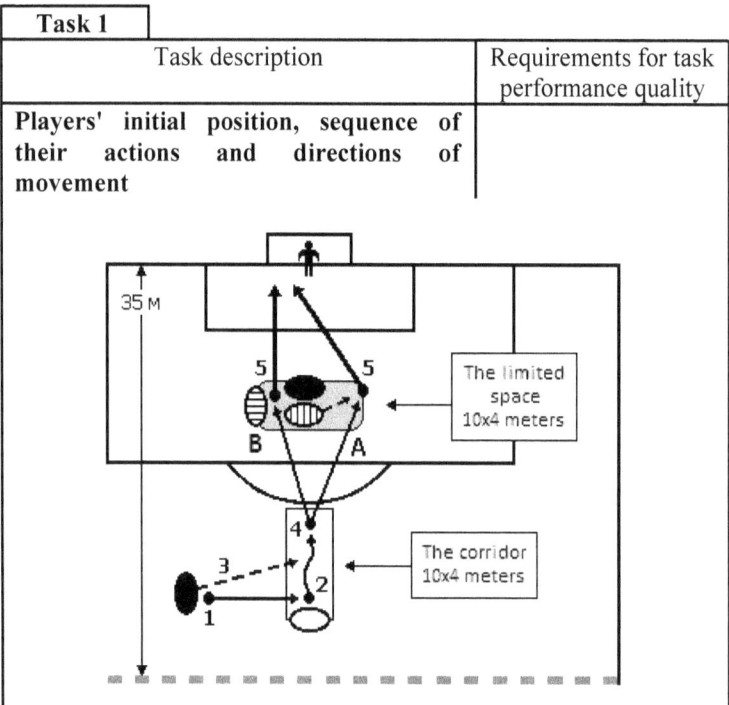	
	A defending player, positioned in the attacking zone, sends the ball to an attacking player, positioned in the «corridor» in the attacking zone, across the pitch surface. An attacking player receives the ball, quickly moves with it through the «corridor» towards the 18-yard box and sends the ball to one of his partners into the limited space in the 18-yard box for shooting on goal.	– a defending player should send the ball to an attacking player precisely at foot; – an attacking player should quickly move with the ball and perform a pass to his partners;

Soccer. Training the «game episodes technique», beginning from coming over the ball in open play

Task 1 continuation	
Task description	Requirements for task performance quality
A defending player, positioned in the attacking zone, begins to move towards an attacking player when the latter firstly touches the ball and tries to prevent him from performing a pass. A defending player positioned in the 18-yard box tries to prevent partners of an attacking player from shooting on goal. **Variants:** a) a defending player sends the ball to an attacking player with a bounce off the pitch surface and on air low-level; b) points of marking of the limited space and the «corridor» and players' initial position are varied; c) the «corridor» is marked in different areas of the attacking zone in parallel to the 18-yard box line;	– partners of an attacking player should try to take most comfortable position for receiving the ball in the limited space timely relative to the moment a pass performance by an attacking player; – an attacking player should quickly identify a partner who is in the best position for receiving the ball; – an attacking player should send the ball to his partners precisely at foot;

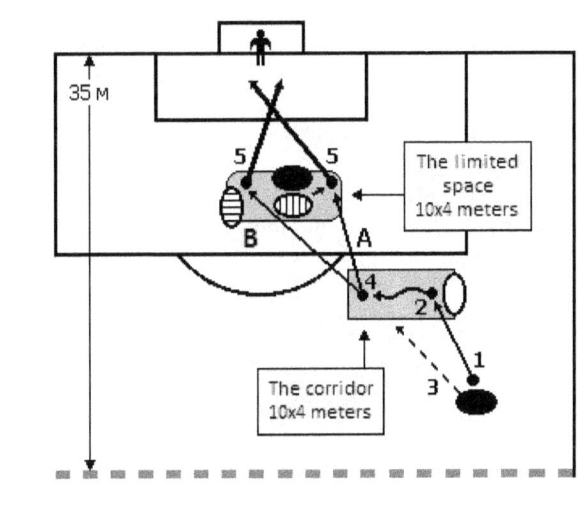

Task 1 continuation	
Task description	Requirements for task performance quality
d) in initial position an attacking player is positioned at some distance from the «corridor» and moves into it in different directions to receive the ball.	– partners of an attacking players should shoot on goal from the limited space exactly;

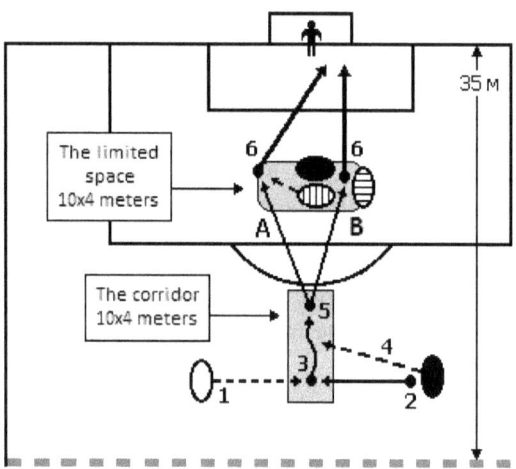

| Notes.
1. A distance between the limited space and the «corridor» varies from 5 to 10 meters.
2. A distance at which a defending player is positioned in the initial position in the attacking zone from an attacking player should be such that he could come up with an attacking player when he performs a pass, beginning the movement when an attacking player makes his first touch of the ball, but at the same time that an attacking player could perform a pass, acting with a maximum speed and precision | – partners of an attacking player should try to send the ball into the area of the goal, unprotected by the goalkeeper, every time |

Task 2	
Task description	Requirements for task performance quality
Players' initial position, sequence of their actions and directions of movement	– a defending player should send the ball to an attacking player precisely at foot;

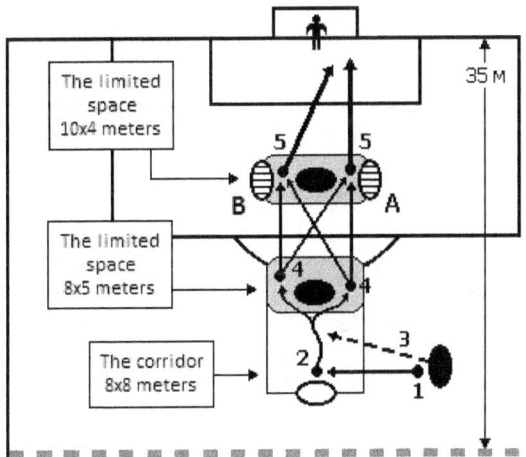

A defending player, positioned in the attacking zone, sends the ball to an attacking player, positioned in the «corridor» in the attacking zone, across the pitch surface. An attacking player receives the ball, quickly moves with it through the «corridor» into the limited space in the attacking zone, beats a defending player to the left or to the right and sends the ball to one of his partners into the limited space in the 18-yard box for shooting on goal. A defending player, positioned in the attacking zone, begins to move towards an attacking player when the latter firstly touches the ball and tries to prevent him from performing a pass.	– an attacking player should quickly move with the ball, beat a defending player and perform a pass to his partners; – partners of an attacking player should try to take most comfortable position for receiving the ball in the limited space timely relative to the moment a pass performance by an attacking player;

Task 2 continuation

Task description	Requirements for task performance quality
A defending player positioned in the limited space in the attacking zone tries to prevent an attacking players from performing a pass. A defending player positioned in the 18-yard box tries to prevent partners of an attacking player from shooting on goal. **Variants:** a) a defending player sends the ball to an attacking player with a bounce off the pitch surface and on air low-level; b) points of marking of limited spaces and the «corridor» and players' initial position are varied; c) the «corridor» is marked in different areas of the attacking zone diagonally to the 18-yard box line; d) in initial position an attacking player is positioned at some distance from the «corridor» and moves into it in different directions to receive the ball. **Notes.** 1. A distance between limited spaces varies from 5 to 10 meters. 2. A distance at which a defending player is positioned in the initial position in the attacking zone from an attacking player should be such that he could come up with an attacking player when he performs a pass, beginning the movement when an attacking player makes his first touch of the ball, but at the same time that an attacking player could perform a pass, acting with a maximum speed and precision	– an attacking player should quickly identify a partner who is in the best position for receiving the ball; – an attacking player should send the ball to his partners precisely at foot; – partners of an attacking players should shoot on goal from the limited space exactly; – partners of an attacking player should try to send the ball into the area of the goal, unprotected by the goalkeeper, every time

Soccer. Training the «game episodes technique», beginning from coming over the ball in open play

Task 3	
Task description	Requirements for task performance quality
Players' initial position, sequence of their actions and directions of movement	– a defending player should send the ball to an attacking player precisely at foot;

[Diagram showing a soccer pitch section with: 35 M marking on the left, "The corridor 10x4 meters" on the right, player positions numbered 1–6, and "The limited space 8x8 meters" area.]

A defending player, positioned in the attacking zone at the «corridor», sends the ball to an attacking player, positioned in the «corridor» in the attacking zone, across the pitch surface. An attacking player receives the ball, quickly moves with it through the «corridor» towards the goal-line and sends the ball to his partner into the limited space in the 18-yard box above a mannequin designating a defending player for shooting on goal. A partner of an attacking player moves into the limited space in the 18-yard box and shoots on goal with a first or a second touch by a foot or a head obligingly.	– an attacking player should quickly move with the ball and perform a pass to his partners; – an attacking player should send the ball to his partner precisely into the limited space with the lowest possible trajectory, yet so that it flew above a mannequin designating a defending player;

151

Task 3 continuation	
Task description	Requirements for task performance quality
A defending player positioned at the «corridor» begins to move towards an attacking player when the latter firstly touches the ball and tries to prevent him from performing a pass. A defending player, positioned behind the back of a partner of an attacking player, begins to move into the limited space in the 18-yard box simultaneously with him and tries to prevent him from shooting on goal. **Variants:** a) a defending player sends the ball to an attacking player with a bounce off the pitch surface and on air low-level; b) points of marking of the limited space and the «corridor» and players' initial position are varied; c) in initial position an attacking player is positioned at some distance from the «corridor» and moves into it in different directions to receive the ball. **Note.** A distance at which a defending player is positioned in the initial position in the attacking zone at the «corridor» from an attacking player should be such that he could come up with an attacking player when he performs a pass, beginning the movement when an attacking player makes his first touch of the ball, but at the same time that an attacking player could perform a pass, acting with a maximum speed and precision	– a partner of an attacking player should begin to move into the 18-yard box timely relative to the moment of the pass performing by an attacking player; – a partner of an attacking player should shoot on goal without reducing the speed of movement; – a partner of an attacking player should shoot on goal with a first or second touch obligingly; – a partner of an attacking player should try to send the ball into the area of the goal, unprotected by the goalkeeper, every time

Soccer. Training the «game episodes technique», beginning from coming over the ball in open play

Task 4	
Task description	Requirements for task performance quality
Players' initial position, sequence of their actions and directions of movement	– a defending player should send the ball to an attacking player precisely at foot;

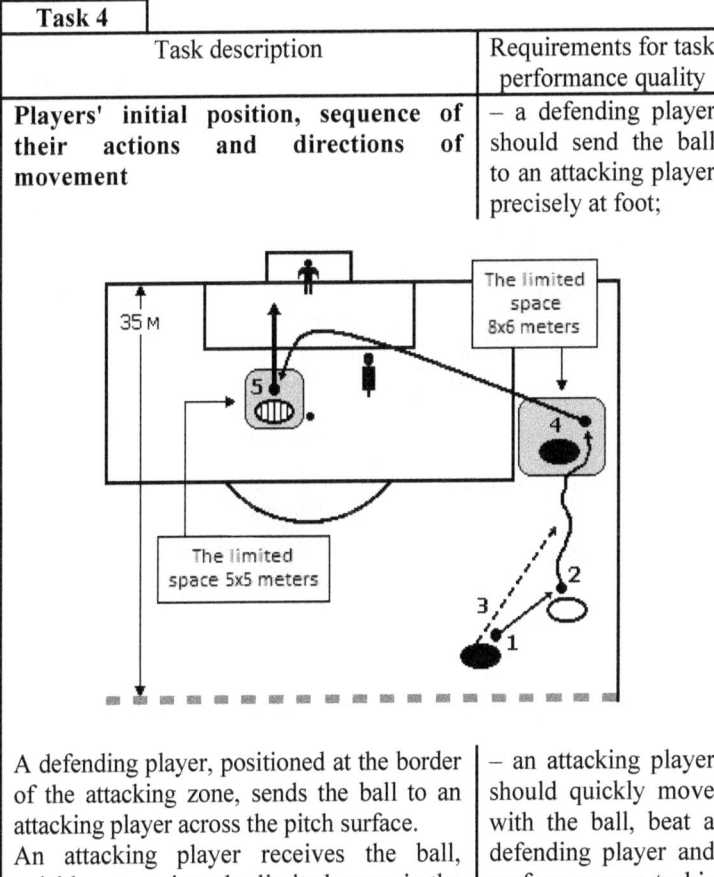

A defending player, positioned at the border of the attacking zone, sends the ball to an attacking player across the pitch surface. An attacking player receives the ball, quickly moves into the limited space in the attacking zone with it, beats a defending player and sends the ball to a partner into the limited space in the 18-yard box above a mannequin designating a defending player for shooting on goal **with a first touch of a foot or a head**. A defending player, positioned at the border of the attacking zone, begins to move towards an attacking player when the latter firstly touches the ball and tries to prevent him from performing a pass.	– an attacking player should quickly move with the ball, beat a defending player and perform a pass to his partner; – an attacking player should send the ball to his partner precisely into the limited space with the lowest possible trajectory, yet so that it flew above a mannequin designating a defending player;

153

Task 4 continuation	
Task description	Requirements for task performance quality
Variants: a) points of marking of limited spaces and players' initial position are varied; b) a defending player sends the ball to an attacking player, moving in various directions in the attacking zone for receiving the ball.	– a partner of an attacking player should shoot on goal with a first touch obligingly;
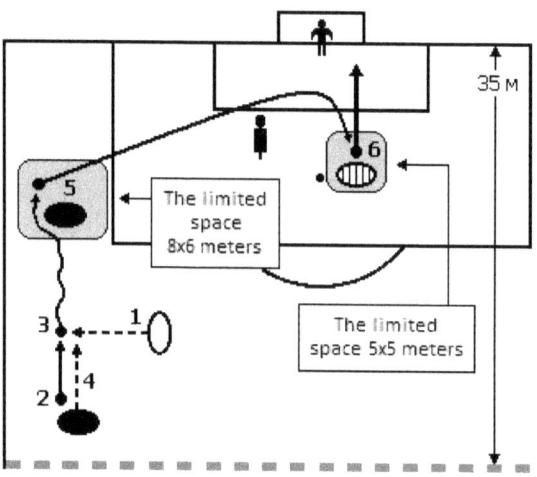	
Note. A distance at which a defending player is positioned in the initial position at the border of the attacking zone from an attacking player should be such that he could come up with an attacking player when he performs a pass, beginning the movement when an attacking player makes his first touch of the ball, but at the same time that an attacking player could perform a pass, acting with a maximum speed and precision	– a partner of an attacking player should try to send the ball into the area of the goal, unprotected by the goalkeeper, every time

Soccer. Training the «game episodes technique», beginning from coming over the ball in open play

Task 5	
Task description	Requirements for task performance quality
Players' initial position, sequence of their actions and directions of movement 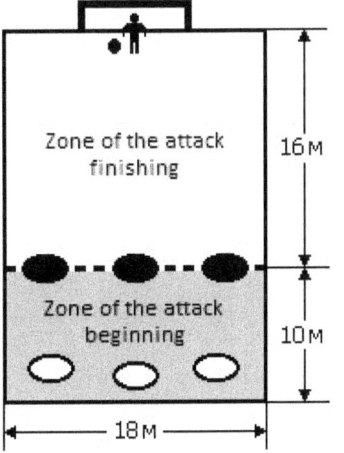 The goalkeeper sends the ball to one of attacking players with a foot or a hand into the zone of the attack beginning with a mounted trajectory. Attacking players try to deliver the ball into the zone of the attack finishing using passes and dribbling and to shoot on goal. When an attacking player firstly touches the ball, defending players begin to move into the zone of the attack beginning and try to prevent attacking players from delivering the ball into the zone of the attack finishing and from shooting on goal. Number of passes in the attack by attacking players is no more than three. **Offsides are given in the zone of the attack finishing**	– having received the ball from the goalkeeper, attacking players should try to deliver the ball into the attacking zone quickly and shoot on goal; – defending players should attack an opponent, who has gained possession of the ball, as fast as possible, forcing him to act amid time and space shortage; – players should perform shots on goal from any, even inconvenient positions; – players should try to use every opportunity to finish off the ball into the net; – while performing shots on goal, players should try to send the ball into the area of the goal, unprotected by the goalkeeper, every time

Task 6	
Task description	Requirements for task performance quality
Four attacking players on two defending players play in two zones, positioned at some distance from each other, providing delivering the ball from zone to zone with a combination of dribbling and passes. Two zones 12 meters wide and 16 meters long are marked on the pitch with long sides opposite to each other 12 meters apart. Goal-areas are marked in each zone no further than 6 meters from the goal-line. Goals are mounted on the opposite short sides of different zones. Two attacking and one defending player act in each zone all the time. Players are prohibited from moving from zone to zone. 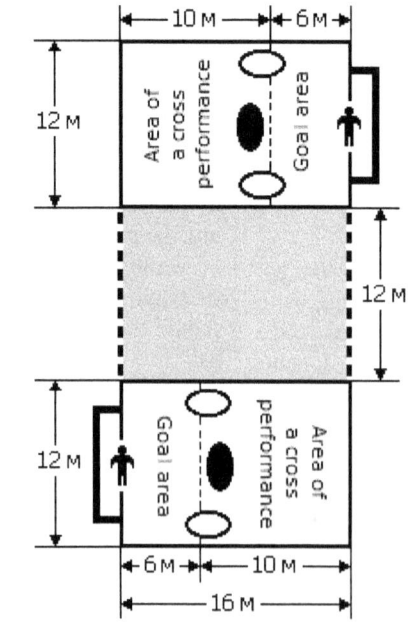	– goalkeepers should put the ball into play without a delay; – defending players should try to intercept the ball or attack an opponent at reception of the ball, entering into physical contact with him; – having received the ball from the goalkeeper, attacking players should try to deliver it to the «area of a cross performance» quickly and pass it into the opposite zone; – attacking players, acting in the same zone, should pass the ball to each other timely and precisely, providing the partner with time for performing a pass into the opposite zone; – having received the ball from the other zone, attacking players should try to quickly finish the attack with a shot on goal;

Soccer. Training the «game episodes technique», beginning from coming over the ball in open play

Task 6 continuation	
Task description	Requirements for task performance quality
Goalkeepers put the ball into play inside the goal-area in the zone where they protect their goal after catching it or when it leaves this area. Two attacking players try to deliver the ball from the goal-area to the «area of a cross performance» with dribbling and passes and pass the ball into the opposite zone for partners to shoot o goal. Number of passes to each other by attacking players who have received the ball from the goalkeeper before sending it to the opposite zone is no more than two. Number of passes to each other by attacking players who have received the ball from the opposite zone before shooting on goal is no more than two. One of defending players tries to prevent attacking players from passing into the opposite zone, while the another – to shoot on goal. While putting the ball into play by the goalkeeper a defending player, acting in this zone, is positioned inside the goal-area. The task for four attacking players is to score as much goals as possible in a definite time. **Offsides are given.** Goal scored with a first touch counts as two. Goal scored at the rebound counts as two. **Variant:** a distance between limited spaces and points of the limited spaces marking are varied	– attacking players, positioned in different zones, should act simultaneously while trying to deliver the ball from zone to zone; – defending players should attack an opponent, who has gained possession of the ball, as fast as possible, forcing him to act amid time and space shortage; – players should perform shots on goal from any, even inconvenient positions; – players should try to use every opportunity to finish off the ball into the net; – while performing shots on goal, players should try to send the ball into the area of the goal, unprotected by the goalkeeper, every time

Task 7	
Task description	Requirements for task performance quality
Four on four play with a «neutral» player acting for the attacking team all the time providing crossing the half-way line by a pass or dribbling and performing shots on goal from the attacking zone. Pitch size: 20 meters wide, 33 meters long. The half-way line, dividing the pitch in attacking and defensive zones, is marked. 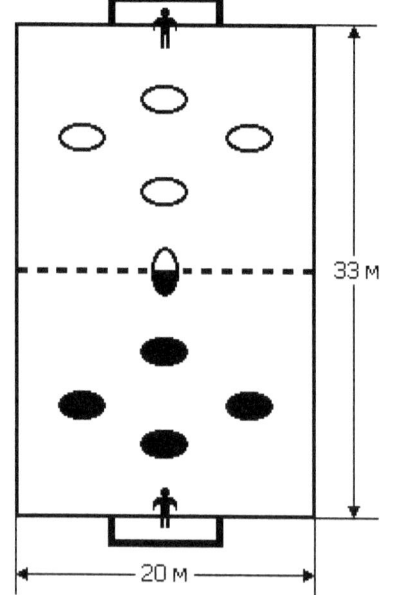 Goalkeepers put the ball into play to their team defensive zone after catching it or when it crosses the goal-line. If the ball leaves the pitch through the sideline players put it into play with hands.	– goalkeepers should put the ball into play without a delay into their team's defensive zone obligingly; – players from the attacking team should try to deliver the ball into the attacking zone quickly and shoot on goal; – players from the attacking team should timely open to receive the ball while performing passes from the defensive into the attacking zone; – defending players should attack an opponent, who has gained possession of the ball, as fast as possible, forcing him to act amid time and space shortage; – players should operate with the ball quickly; – players should try to use every opportunity to finish off the ball into the net;

Soccer. Training the «game episodes technique», beginning from coming over the ball in open play

Task 7 continuation	
Task description	Requirements for task performance quality
Players from the attacking team try to deliver the ball from the defensive into the attacking zone by means of **a pass or dribbling across the half-way line** and to shoot on goal from this zone. Number of passes by attacking players during the attack is no more than three in the defensive zone and no more than two in the attacking zone. Number of touches by each player is not limited. Players from the defending team try to prevent players from the attacking team from delivering the ball into the attacking zone and shoot on goal while positioning in the opponents' defensive zone when their goalkeeper puts the ball into play. Players are prohibited from crossing the half-way line before it is crossed by the ball. Corners are not awarded. **Offsides are given.** Goal scored with a first touch counts as two. Goal scored at the rebound counts as two. Play time in one repeat – 5 minutes. **Variant:** goals are dislocated relative to each other every which way along the goal-line	– while performing shots on goal, players should try to send the ball into the area of the goal, unprotected by the goalkeeper, every time

Drills in which shots on goal from the outside of the 18-yard box are performed

Task 1	
Task description	Requirements for task performance quality
Players' initial position, sequence of their actions and directions of movement	
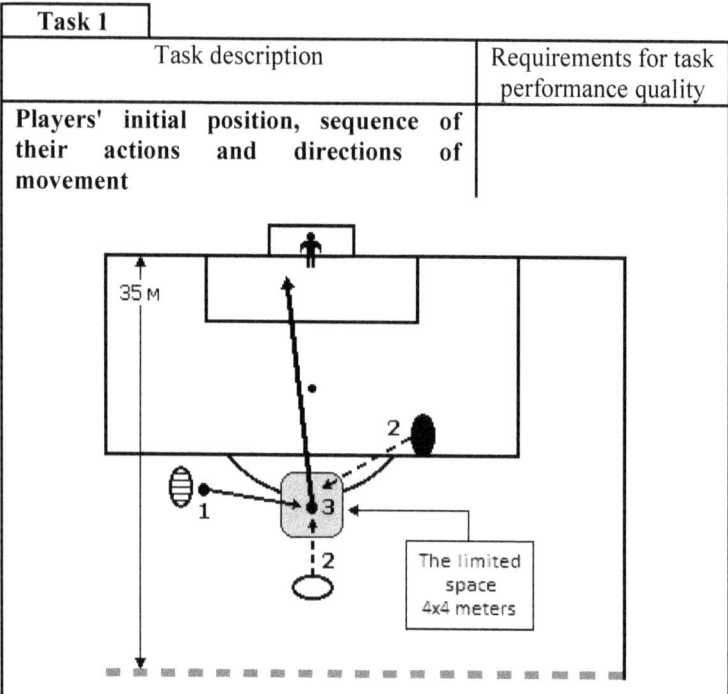	
A partner of an attacking player sends the ball into the limited space across the pitch surface. An attacking player moves quickly into the limited space and shoots on goal **with a first touch obligingly**. At the moment of a pass performing by an attacking player's partner a defending player begins to move into the limited space and tries to prevent an attacking player from shooting on goal, **acting in the supporting position**.	– a partner of an attacking player should send the ball into the limited space precisely and with the necessary speed; – an attacking player should begin to move into the limited space timely relative to the moment of the pass performing by a partner;

Task 1 continuation	
Task description	Requirements for task performance quality
Variants: a) a partner of an attacking player sends the ball into the limited space with a bounce off the pitch surface; b) points of the limited space marking in the area no further than 25 meters from the 18-yard box line and the players' initial position are varied.	– an attacking player should shoot on goal from the limited space exactly; – an attacking player should try to send the ball on target every time
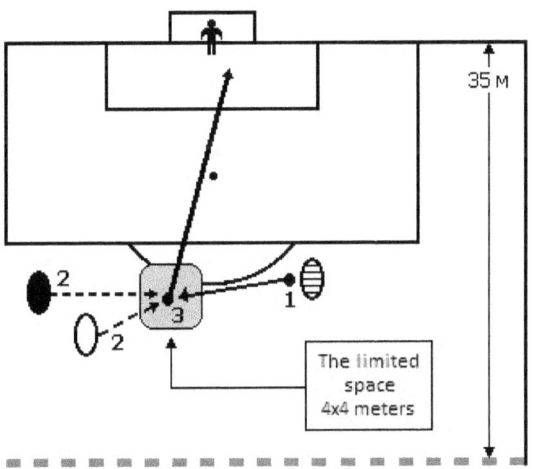	
Note. A distance at which a defending player is positioned in the initial position from the limited space should be such that he could come up with an attacking player when the latter shoots on goal, beginning the movement when a partner of an attacking player performs a pass, but at the same time that an attacking player could shoot on goal from the limited space, acting with a maximum speed	

Task 2	
Task description	Requirements for task performance quality
Players' initial position, sequence of their actions and directions of movement	
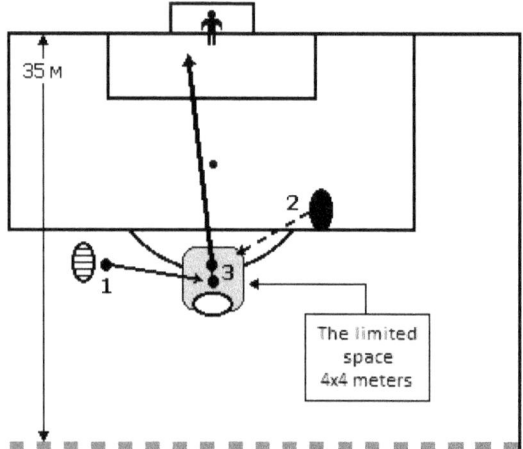	
A partner of an attacking player sends the ball into the limited space across the pitch surface. An attacking player receives the ball and shoots on goal from the limited space **with a second touch obligingly.** At the moment of a pass performing by an attacking player's partner a defending player begins to move into the limited space and tries to prevent an attacking player from shooting on goal, **acting in the supporting position.** **Variants:** a) a partner of an attacking player sends the ball into the limited space with a bounce off the pitch surface;	– a partner of an attacking player should send the ball into the limited space precisely and with the necessary speed; – in cases when an attacking player is positioned in the initial position beyond the limited space, a defending player should perform a pass to an attacking player timely relative to the moment when the latter begins to move into the limited space;

Task 2 continuation	
Task description	Requirements for task performance quality
b) points of the limited space marking in the area no further than 25 meters from the 18-yard box line and the players' initial position are varied; c) in initial position an attacking player is positioned beyond from the limited space and moves into it in different directions to receive the ball.	– an attacking player should shoot on goal from the limited space exactly;

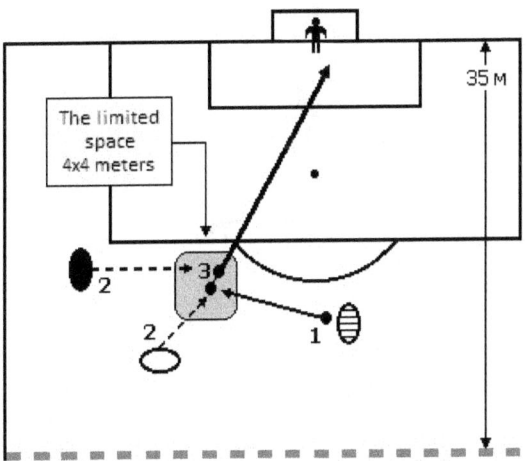

Note. A distance at which a defending player is positioned in the initial position from the limited space should be such that he could come up with an attacking player when the latter shoots on goal, beginning the movement when a partner of an attacking player performs a pass, but at the same time that an attacking player could shoot on goal from the limited space, acting with a maximum speed	– having received the ball, an attacking player should shoot on goal with a second touch without a delay and with a maximum speed; – an attacking player should try to send the ball on target every time

Task 3		
	Task description	Requirements for task performance quality
	Players' initial position, sequence of their actions and directions of movement	

[Diagram: 35 m marking; goal with goalkeeper; limited space 4x4 meters with players numbered 2, 3, 4, 5, 6 and another 5]

A partner of an attacking player sends the ball to an attacking player across the pitch surface. An attacking player receives the ball, quickly moves with it towards the limited space and passes the ball to the second partner. The second partner of an attacking player sends the ball into the limited space across the pitch surface **with a first touch.** An attacking player moves into the limited space and shoots on goal **with a first or a second touch.** At the moment of a pass performing by the attacking player's second partner a defending player begins to move into the limited space and tries to prevent an attacking player from shooting on goal.	– a partner of an attacking player should send the ball to an attacking player precisely at foot; – in cases when an attacking player moves for receiving the ball, his partner should perform a pass to him timely relative to the moment when he begins to move; – an attacking player should quickly move towards the limited space with the ball, perform a pass to a

Soccer. Training the «game episodes technique», beginning from coming over the ball in open play

Task 3 continuation	
Task description	Requirements for task performance quality
Variants: a) points of the limited space marking in the area no further than 25 meters from the 18-yard box line and the players' initial position are varied; c) the first partner of an attacking player sends the ball to an attacking player, moving in various directions in the attacking zone for receiving the ball.	partner and shoot on goal; – the second partner of an attacking player should send the ball into the limited space precisely and with the necessary speed;

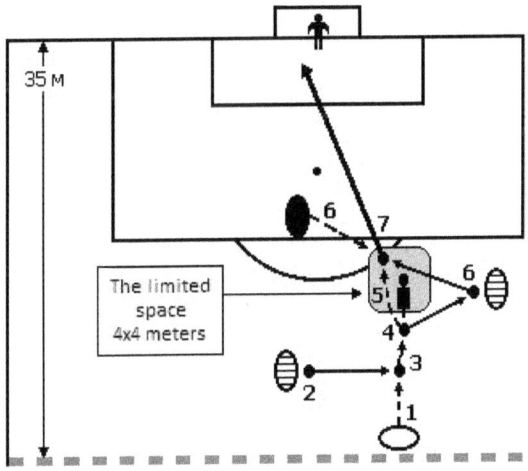

Note. A distance at which a defending player is positioned in the initial position from the limited space should be such that he could come up with an attacking player when the latter shoots on goal, beginning the movement when the second partner of an attacking player performs a pass, but at the same time that an attacking player could shoot on goal from the limited space, acting with a maximum speed	– an attacking player should shoot on goal from the limited space exactly; – an attacking player should try to send the ball on target every time

Task 4	
Task description	Requirements for task performance quality
Players' initial position, sequence of their actions and directions of movement	

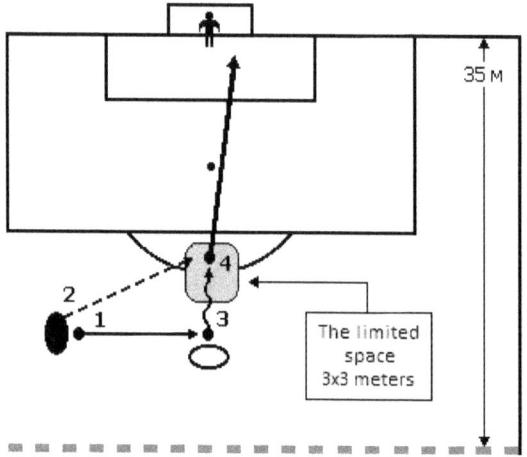

A defending player sends the ball to an attacking player in the attacking zone across the pitch surface. An attacking player receives the ball, quickly moves into the limited space with it and shoots on goal. Having performed a pass, a defending player begins to move into the limited space and tries to prevent an attacking player from shooting on goal. **Variants:** a) a defending player sends the ball to an attacking player with a bounce off the pitch surface and on air low-level; b) points of the limited space marking in the area no further than 25 meters from the 18-yard box line and the players' initial position are varied;	– a defending player should send the ball to an attacking player precisely at foot; – in cases when an attacking player is positioned in the initial position beyond the 18-yard box, a defending player should perform a pass to an attacking player towards the 18-yard box line timely relative to the moment when the latter begins to move into the 18-yard box;

Soccer. Training the «game episodes technique», beginning from coming over the ball in open play

Task 4 continuation	
Task description	Requirements for task performance quality
c) a defending player sends the ball to an attacking player, moving in various directions in the attacking zone for receiving the ball.	– an attacking player should quickly move into the limited space with the ball and shoot on goal;

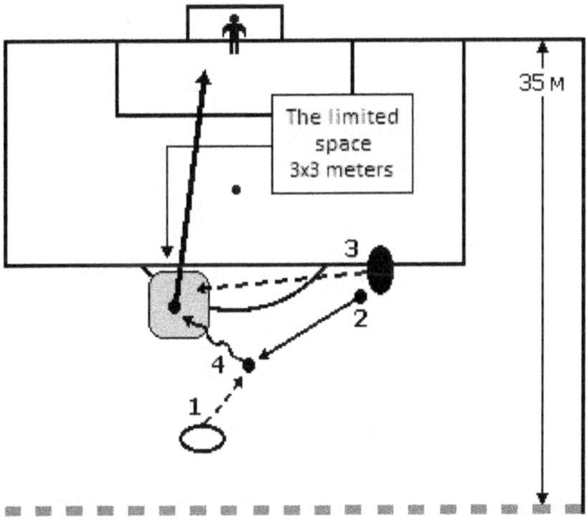

[Diagram: A field layout showing a goal at the top with a goalkeeper figure. Below is "The limited space 3x3 meters". Players numbered 1, 2, 3, 4 are shown with movement arrows. The distance marked is 35 м.]

Note. A distance at which a defending player is positioned in the initial position from the limited space should be such that he could come up with an attacking player when the latter shoots on goal, beginning the movement after performing a pass, but at the same time that an attacking player could shoot on goal from the limited space, acting with a maximum speed and precision	– an attacking player should shoot on goal also with a physical contact with a defending player; – an attacking player should shoot on goal from the limited space exactly; – an attacking player should try to send the ball on target every time

167

Task 5

Task description	Requirements for task performance quality
Players' initial position, sequence of their actions and directions of movement	

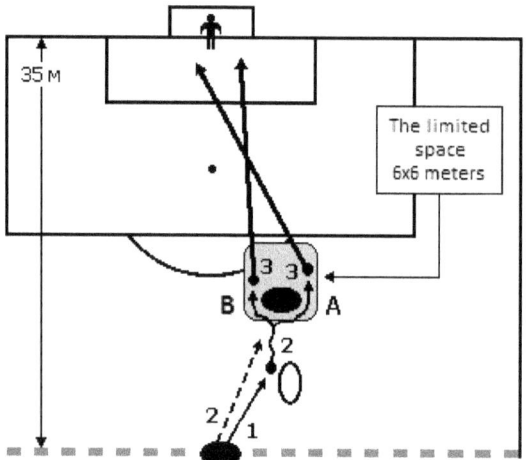

A defending player, positioned on the border of the attacking zone, sends the ball to an attacking player across the pitch surface. An attacking player receives the ball, quickly moves with it into the limited space, beats a defending player to the left or to the right and shoots on goal. A defending player positioned on the border of the attacking zone begins to move into the limited space when an attacking player makes his first touch of the ball and tries to prevent an attacking player from shooting on goal. **Variants:** a) a defending player sends the ball to an attacking player with a bounce off the pitch surface and on air low-level;	– a defending player should send the ball to an attacking player precisely at foot; – in cases when an attacking player moves for receiving the ball, a defending player should perform a pass to him timely relative to the moment when he begins to move; – an attacking player should quickly move into the limited space with the ball, beat a defending player and shoot on goal;

Soccer. Training the «game episodes technique», beginning from coming over the ball in open play

Task 5 continuation	
Task description	Requirements for task performance quality
b) points of the limited space marking in the area no further than 25 meters from the 18-yard box line and the players' initial position are varied; c) a defending player sends the ball to an attacking player, moving in various directions in the attacking zone for receiving the ball.	– an attacking player should shoot on goal from the limited space exactly; – an attacking player should try to send the ball on target every time

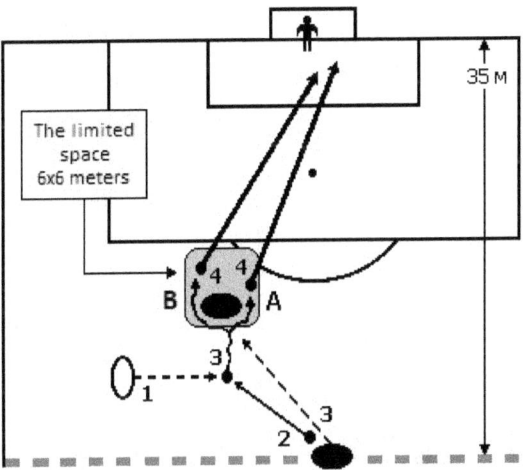

Note. A distance at which a defending player is positioned in the initial position on the border of the attacking zone from an attacking player should be such that he could come up with an attacking player when he shoots on goal, beginning the movement when an attacking player makes his first touch of the ball, but at the same time that an attacking player could shoot on goal from the limited space, acting with a maximum speed and precision

Task 6	
Task description	Requirements for task performance quality
Two on two play with a «neutral» player acting for the attacking team all the time, providing all players acting in the middle zone. Pitch size: 15 meters wide, 40 meters long. Middle zone 8 meters long and the goal area not far than 6 meters from the goal-line are marked on the pitch. Players are acting in the middle zone all the time. 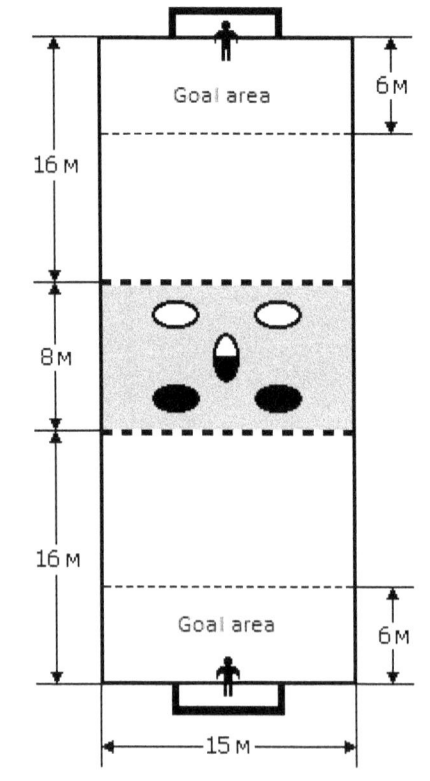	– in a short period after a signal for putting the ball into play players should receive the ball from the goalkeeper; – players should use various techniques of opening for receiving the ball from the goalkeeper and partners in the most comfortable position; – while performing passes by the goalkeeper players from the defending team should try to intercept the ball or attack a rival player at reception of the ball, entering into physical contact with him; – goalkeepers and players should pass the ball to the partner timely and precisely, providing him with time for performing a shot on goal; – players should interact with their partners quickly;

Soccer. Training the «game episodes technique», beginning from coming over the ball in open play

Task 6 continuation	
Task description	Requirements for task performance quality
On signal goalkeepers put the ball into play to the middle zone of the pitch from the goal-area after catching it or when it has left the field through the goal-line or sidelines. Players from the attacking team try to outplay players from the defending team and shoot on goal from the middle zone. Number of passes by outfield players during the attack is no more than three. Players from the attacking team are permitted to finish off the ball into the net beyond the middle zone. Goal scored in such manner counts as two. Players from the defending team try to prevent attacking players to shoot on goal. Corners are not awarded. Offsides are not given. Goal scored with a first touch counts as two. Play time in one repeat – 5 minutes. **Variant:** three on three play with the «neutral» player acting all the time for the attacking team on the pitch 20 meters wide	– players from the defending team should attack an opponent, who has gained possession of the ball, as fast as possible, forcing him to act amid time and space shortage; – players should handle the ball quickly, and especially fast perform the strike motion while shooting on goal; – players should perform shots on goal from any, even inconvenient positions; – players should try to use every opportunity to finish off the ball into the net; – while performing shots on goal, players should try to send the ball into the area of the goal, unprotected by the goalkeeper, every time

Task 7	
Task description	Requirements for task performance quality
Three on three play providing two players acting in the defensive zone and one in the attacking zone all the time. Pitch size: 15 meters wide, 23 meters long. Three zones are marked on the pitch: attacking and defensive 7 meters long each and the middle 9 meters long. In each team two players act in their team defensive zone, and one –in the attacking zone all the time. Players are prohibited from moving from zone to zone. 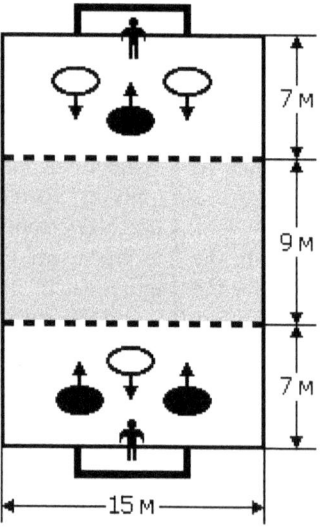 Goalkeepers put the ball into play to their team defensive zone after catching it or when it crosses the goal-line and sidelines.	– goalkeepers should put the ball into play without a delay; – a player from the defending team acting in the opponents' defensive zone should attack a rival player to whom the ball is passed as quick as possible, forcing him to act amid time and space shortage; – players should pass the ball to the partner timely and precisely, providing him with time for performing a shot on goal; – player from the attacking team, acting in the attacking zone, should reduce the visibility for the goalkeeper and change the direction of the ball when his partners shoot on goal; – attacking players should shoot on goal also with a first touch;

Soccer. Training the «game episodes technique», beginning from coming over the ball in open play

Task 7 continuation	
Task description	Requirements for task performance quality
Two players from the attacking team acting in the defensive zone try to outplay a player from the defending team and shoot on goal from this zone. Number of passes by outfield players during the attack is no more than two. Player from the attacking team, acting in the attacking zone, tries to reduce the visibility for the goalkeeper, change the direction of the ball to the goal and finish off the ball into the net. Player from the defending team, acting in the opponent's defensive zone, tries to tackle the ball and shoot on goal or pass to partners in his team defensive zone. Corners are not awarded. Offsides are not given. Goal scored with a first touch counts as two. Goal scored at the rebound counts as two. Play time in one repeat – 5 minutes. **Variants:** a) goals are dislocated relative to each other every which way along the goal-line; b) player are permitted to shoot on goal from the middle zone with a first touch in cases when the ball bounces into these zone from the goal, goalkeeper and players	– players should handle the ball quickly, and especially fast perform the strike motion while shooting on goal; – players should perform shots on goal from any, even inconvenient positions; – a player from the attacking team, acting in the attacking zone, should try to use every opportunity to finish off the ball into the net; – while performing shots on goal, players should try to send the ball into the area of the goal, unprotected by the goalkeeper, every time

CHAPTER 5. PERFECTION OF THE «GAME EPISODES TECHNIQUE» IN THE MIDDLE AND AND DEFENSIVE ZONES

Characteristics of the drills construction

Principal task that should be solved while training the «game episodes technique» in the middle and defensive zones is the perfection of the technique of:
– the quick delivery of the ball to the shooting position;
– certain actions with the ball performed during delivery of the ball to the shooting position.

While constructing drills providing the performance of attacking actions with goalscoring, we have to consider several provisions.

First. There are no specific distinctions in the technique of actions with the ball in the middle and in the defensive zones, and so drills for training the «game episodes technique» in these zones are similar in construction and differ only in points of the attack beginning and its longevity.

Second. Quickness and precision of the ball delivery to the shooting position take central stage in drills for perfection of the «game episodes technique» in the middle and defensive zones.

Time of the attacks undergoing should be:
– from 5 to 20 seconds in case attacks begin 40 to 80 meters from the defending team's goal-line;
– no more than 25 seconds in case attacks begin 80 meters and more from the defending team's goal-line;

Third. The following actions may be performed to cover the distance towards the opponent's goal (either separately and in combination):

– movements with the ball at various distance;
– passes at short distance, performed quickly and in progressive direction;
– passes for long distances.

In case there is an opponent on the way of a player moving with the ball on a high speed, the quickness of attack depends on the players' ability to change the direction of the movement with the ball timely and without reducing the speed of movement.

The quickness of covering the space with a short passes may be achieved if the ball is sent to players going forward, while a player who has received the ball moves maintaining the speed of the attack. Players should virtually act on the principle of batoon: having come over the ball, quickly move with it towards the opponents' goal and pass it to a partner, who is also moving forward.

Success of covering the space with short passes amid the high overcrowding of players in relatively small area of the pitch is largely predefined by an ability to **play two quick touches,** when a bunch of actions «a reception and a pass» is performed with the same foot, and the second touch follows the first without a delay (with a maximum speed).

It needs not much more time for performing a pass with a dispatched second touch than with a first one, yet it is enough for a player to change the direction of a pass if necessary.

While performing passes at long distances the ball may be sent directly to a player or on his way into the certain area of the pitch. In both cases the ball flies for sufficiently long time, and defending players have an opportunity to prepare for its interception.

In this regard one of tasks while training the «game episodes technique», in which the ball is passed at long distances with a high speed, is the perfection of technique of reception such passes by attacking players amid the opponent's countering with the following continuation of attacking actions.

Coming over the ball after passes at long distances may be performed in two ways, namely when a player:

– receives the ball back to the opponent's goal (in static position or with coming up to the ball);

– moves into the area of the pitch, which the ball is sent into, at various angles relative to the direction of a pass.

Fourth. Quick delivery of the ball at the shooting position suggests actions with a maximum output. Since certain players have to cross long distances during attacks beginning in the middle and defensive zones, the question that has to be answered is the ultimate individual longevity of a work with a maximum output, after which players are still able to act with the ball quickly and accurately.

It has to be noted while constructing drills, that each player has his own distance, covering which with a maximum power he is able to act with the ball quickly and accurately, and the range of their actions with such an output should be defined for players accordingly.

Necessary pauses for recovery should be provided for players to perform each repeat of a task with a maximum output exactly.

Fifth. Players may be encouraged to quickly deliver the ball at the shooting position by means of the following methodological techniques:

– introduction of elements of competition;

– managing a drill so that players, performing attacking actions, are followed by an opponent.

Sixth. In gaming drills players should begin attacking actions after a tackle or an interception of the ball at the same distance from the defending team's goal-line as the one at which goalscoring attacks begin after a tackle or an interception in competitive matches, and namely from areas 60-70 and 75-95 meters from the defending team's goal-line.

Following are examples of drills for perfection of the «game episodes technique» in the middle and defensive zones.

Drills in which space is covered by means of dribbling

Task 1		
Task description		Requirements for task performance quality
Players' initial position, sequence of their actions and directions of movement An attacking player is positioned in the «corridor» 4-5 meters from the ball back to the limited space. 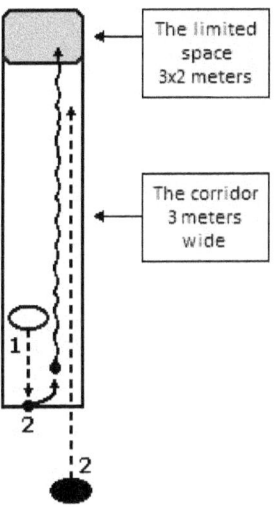 An attacking player quickly moves to the ball, turn round and moves with the ball through the «corridor» into the limited space. When an attacking player makes his first touch of the ball, a defending player begins to move towards an attacking player and tries to prevent him from delivering the ball into the limited space.		– an attacking player should quickly perform a U-turn; – an attacking player should perform the second touch of the ball soon after the first touch obligingly; – an attacking player should begin the starting speed-up with the ball with a maximum power; – while beginning the starting speed-up, an attacking player should act with the ball accurately; – an attacking player should quickly deliver the ball into the limited space without letting the ball leave the «corridor»

Task 1 continuation	
Task description	Requirements for task performance quality
Variants: a) length of the «corridor» is varied; b) an attacking player is positioned beyond the «corridor» in initial position so that he could turn 90 degrees and more with the ball after moving to it in various directions; *[Diagram: a corridor 3 meters wide leading to a limited space 3x2 meters, with positions marked 1 and 2]* c) width of the «corridor» is decreased to 2 meters. **Note.** A distance at which a defending player is positioned in the initial position from the ball should be such that he could be close enough to an attacking player, beginning the movement when the latter touches the ball, but at the same time that an attacking player could deliver the ball into the limited space, acting with a maximum speed and precision	

Task 2	
Task description	Requirements for task performance quality
Players' initial position, sequence of their actions and directions of movement
An attacking player is positioned in the «corridor» at its entry face to the defending player and back to the limited space.

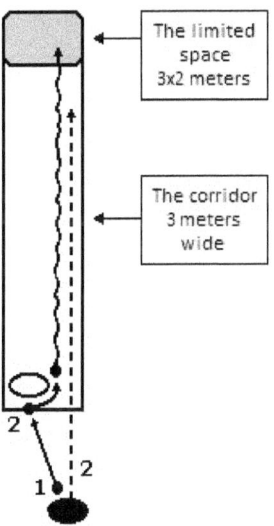

A defending player sends the ball to an attacking player into the «corridor» across the pitch surface.
An attacking player receives the ball with a U-turn and quickly moves with the it through the «corridor» into the limited space.
When an attacking player makes his first touch of the ball, a defending player begins to move towards an attacking player and tries to prevent him from delivering the ball into the limited space. | – a defending player should pass the ball to an attacking player precisely at foot;
– an attacking player should quickly perform a U-turn;
– an attacking player should perform the second touch of the ball soon after the first touch obligingly;
– an attacking player should begin the starting speed-up with the ball with a maximum power;
– while beginning the starting speed-up, an attacking player should act with the ball accurately;
– an attacking player should quickly deliver the ball into the limited space without letting the ball leave the «corridor» |

Task 2 continuation	
Task description	Requirements for task performance quality
Variants: a) length of the «corridor» is varied; b) an attacking player is positioned beyond the «corridor» in initial position so that he could turn 90 degrees and more with the ball after moving to the point of receiving the ball in various directions; *[Diagram: The limited space 3x2 meters; The corridor 3 meters wide]* c) width of the «corridor» is decreased to 2 meters. **Note.** A distance at which a defending player is positioned in the initial position from the point of receiving the ball by an attacking player should be such that he could be close enough to an attacking player, beginning the movement when the latter touches the ball, but at the same time that an attacking player could deliver the ball into the limited space, acting with a maximum speed and precision	

Task 3	
Task description	Requirements for task performance quality
Players' initial position, sequence of their actions and directions of movement An attacking player is positioned in the «corridor» at its entry face to the defending player, positioned beyond the «corridor», and back to the limited space. 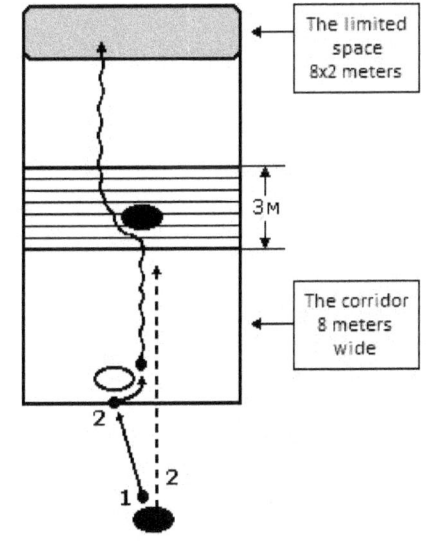 A defending player, positioned beyond the «corridor», sends the ball to an attacking player into the «corridor» across the pitch surface. An attacking player receives the ball with a U-turn and quickly moves with it through the «corridor» into the limited space, beating a defending player, positioned in the zone crossing the «corridor», on course of his movement.	– a defending player should pass the ball to an attacking player precisely at foot; – an attacking player should quickly perform a U-turn; – an attacking player should perform the second touch of the ball soon after the first touch obligingly; – an attacking player should begin the starting speed-up with the ball with a maximum power; – while beginning the starting speed-up, an attacking player should act with the ball accurately; – an attacking player should quickly deliver the ball into the limited space; – an attacking player should lower the speed of movement while beating an opponent to a lesser possible extent

Task 3 continuation	
Task description	Requirements for task performance quality
When an attacking player makes his first touch of the ball, a defending player, positioned beyond the «corridor», begins to move towards an attacking player and tries to prevent him from delivering the ball into the limited space. A defending player, positioned in the zone crossing the «corridor», tries to prevent an attacking player from delivering the ball into the limited space. **Variants:** a) length of the «corridor» is varied; b) point of marking of the zone crossing the «corridor» is varied relative to the initial position of an attacking player (closer-further); c) an attacking player is positioned beyond the «corridor» in initial position so that he could turn 90 degrees and more with the ball after moving to the point of receiving the ball in various directions. **Notes.** 1. A distance at which a defending player is positioned in the initial position beyond the «corridor» from the point of receiving the ball by an attacking player should be such that he could be close enough to an attacking player, beginning the movement when the latter touches the ball, but at the same time that an attacking player could deliver the ball into the limited space, acting with a maximum speed and precision. 2. A defending player, positioned in the zone crossing the «corridor», acts in this zone only	

Task 4

Task description	Requirements for task performance quality
Players' initial position, sequence of their actions and directions of movement An attacking player is positioned in the «corridor» at its entry face to the defending player, positioned beyond the «corridor», and back to the limited space. 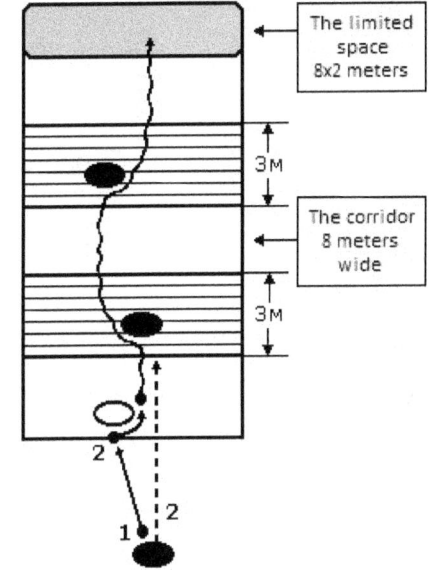 A defending player, positioned beyond the «corridor», sends the ball to an attacking player into the «corridor» across the pitch surface. An attacking player receives the ball with a U-turn and quickly moves with it through the «corridor» into the limited space, beating two defending players, positioned in two zones crossing the «corridor», on course of his movement.	– a defending player should pass the ball to an attacking player precisely at foot; – an attacking player should quickly perform a U-turn; – an attacking player should perform the second touch of the ball soon after the first touch obligingly; – an attacking player should begin the starting speed-up with the ball with a maximum power; – while beginning the starting speed-up, an attacking player should act with the ball accurately; – an attacking player should quickly deliver the ball into the limited space; – an attacking player should lower the speed of movement while beating his opponents to a lesser possible extent

Task 4 continuation	
Task description	Requirements for task performance quality
When an attacking player makes his first touch of the ball, a defending player, positioned beyond the «corridor», begins to move towards an attacking player and tries to prevent him from delivering the ball into the limited space. Defending players, positioned in zones crossing the «corridor», try to prevent an attacking player from delivering the ball into the limited space. **Variants:** a) length of the «corridor» is varied; b) points of marking of zones crossing the «corridor» are varied relative to the initial position of an attacking player (closer-further); c) an attacking player is positioned beyond the «corridor» in initial position so that he could turn 90 degrees and more with the ball after moving to the point of receiving the ball in various directions. **Notes.** 1. A distance at which a defending player is positioned in the initial position beyond the «corridor» from the point of receiving the ball by an attacking player should be such that he could be close enough to an attacking player, beginning the movement when the latter touches the ball, but at the same time that an attacking player could deliver the ball into the limited space, acting with a maximum speed and precision. 2. Defending players, positioned in zones crossing the «corridor», act in their zone only	

Drills in which space is covered by means of passes with a second touch, performed immediately after the first touch

Task 1	
Task description	Requirements for task performance quality
Three on three play without the goal with two «neutral» players acting all the time for the attacking team. Pitch size: 12 meters wide, 12 meters long. Attacking and defensive zones, 4 meters long each, are marked on the pitch. 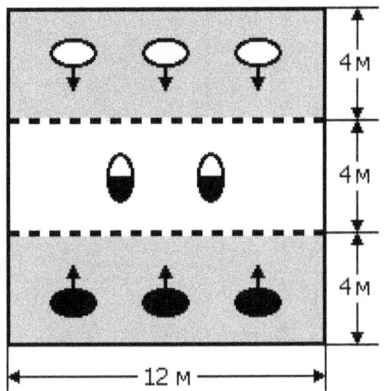 Players from the attacking team try to deliver the ball from the defensive to the attacking zone, **passing it with a second touch, performed without delay after a first with a same foot,** and fix (stop) the ball with a second touch in the attacking zone.	– players from the attacking team should try to deliver the ball into the attacking zone quickly and shoot on goal; – players from the defending team should attack a player, who has gained possession of the ball, as fast as possible, forcing him to act amid time and space shortage; – players from the attacking team should open to receive the ball timely relative to the moment when their partner receives the ball; – players should perform passes as soon after a first touch of the ball as possible;

Task 1 continuation	
Task description	Requirements for task performance quality
In case players perform passes with delay between first and second touches or perform them with different feet, the right to possess the ball goes to opponents. Number of passes in the attack is no more than five. If the ball leaves the pitch through the sideline players put it into play by a pass with a foot. Corners are not awarded. Offsides are not given. **Variant:** three on three play without the goal and with the «neutral» player acting all the time for the attacking team	– players should send the ball to their partners precisely at foot

Task 2		
	Task description	Requirements for task performance quality
	Three on three play with two «neutral» players acting all the time for the attacking team. Pitch size: 15 meters wide, 15 meters long. The half-way line, dividing the pitch in attacking and defensive zones, is marked. 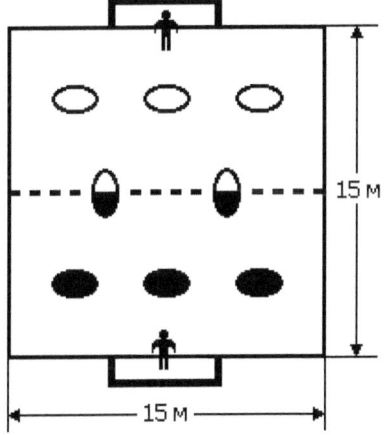 After catching the ball or when it crosses the goal-line goalkeepers put it into play into the defensive zone of their team. Players from the attacking team try to deliver the ball from the defensive into the attacking zone, **passing it with a second touch performed without delay after a first touch with the same foot, and to shoot on goal with a second touch, performed without delay after a first touch with the same foot.**	– goalkeepers should put the ball into play without a delay; – players from the attacking team should try to deliver the ball into the attacking zone quickly and shoot on goal; – players from the defending team should attack a player, who has gained possession of the ball, as fast as possible, forcing him to act amid time and space shortage; – players from the attacking team should open to receive the ball timely relative to the moment when their partner receives the ball; – players should perform passes and shoot on goal as soon after a first touch of the ball as possible; – players should send the ball to their partners precisely at foot;

Task 2 continuation	
Task description	Requirements for task performance quality
In case players perform passes and shots on goal with delay between first and second touches or perform them with different feet, the right to possess the ball goes to opponents. Number of passes in the attack is no more than five. If the ball leaves the pitch through the sideline players put it into play by a pass with a foot. Corners are not awarded. Offsides are not given. **Variant:** three on three play with the «neutral» player acting all the time for the attacking team	– while performing shots on goal, players should try to send the ball into the area of the goal, unprotected by the goalkeeper, every time

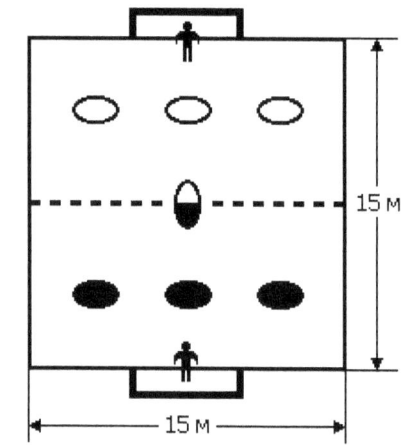

Soccer. Training the «game episodes technique», beginning from coming over the ball in open play

Task 3		
	Task description	Requirements for task performance quality
	Four on four play with two «neutral» players acting all the time for the attacking team. Pitch size: 12 meters wide, 25 meters long. Three zones are marked on the pitch: attacking and defensive 10 meters long each and the middle 5 meters long. In each team two players act in their team defensive zone, and one – in the attacking zone all the time. One «neutral» player acting in the defensive area, and another – in the attacking zone all the time. Players are prohibited from moving from zone to zone. 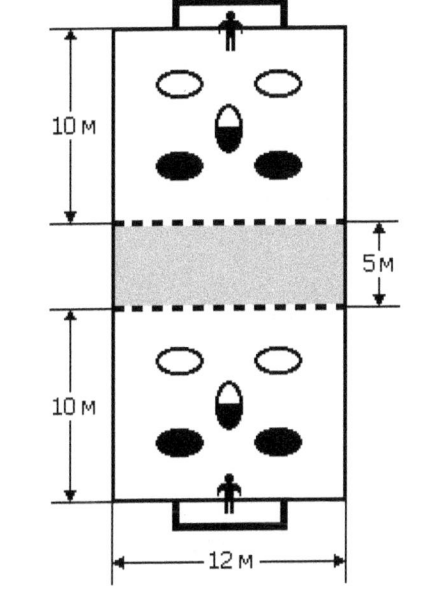	– goalkeepers should put the ball into play without a delay; – players from the attacking team should try to deliver the ball into the attacking zone quickly and shoot on goal; – players from the defending team should attack a player, who has gained possession of the ball, as fast as possible, forcing him to act amid time and space shortage; – players from the attacking team, positioned in their defensive zone, should perform passes to each other and into the attacking zone as soon after a first touch of the ball as possible; – players from the attacking team, positioned in the attacking zones, should try to take most comfortable position for receiving the ball every time;

Task 3 continuation	
Task description	Requirements for task performance quality
After catching the ball or when it crosses the goal-line goalkeepers put it into play into the defensive zone of their team. Players from the attacking team try to beat their opponents and deliver the ball to their partners in the attacking zone, **passing it with a second touch, performed without delay after a first touch with the same foot.** Players from the attacking team, positioned in the attacking zone, try to beat players from the defensive team and shoot goal, acting with the ball without limitation in number of touches of the ball by each player. In case players from the attacking team, positioned in their defensive zone, perform passes with delay between first and second touches or perform them with different feet, the right to possess the ball goes to opponents. Number of passes by players during the attack is no more than three in the defensive zone and no more than three in the attacking zone. If the ball leaves the pitch through the sideline players put it into play by a pass with a foot. Corners are not awarded. Offsides are not given	– players should send the ball to their partners precisely at foot; – while performing shots on goal, players should try to send the ball into the area of the goal, unprotected by the goalkeeper, every time

Drills in which space is covered by means of combination of dribbling and short and medium passes

Task 1	
Task description	Requirements for task performance quality
Players' initial position, sequence of their actions and directions of movement	– an attacking player should receive the ball from a defending player with the drifting; – an attacking player, who has received the ball from a defending player, should perform a second touch of the ball very quickly after a first touch and begin to perform starting speed-up with the ball powerfully; – attacking players should send the ball to each other so that it is comfortable to receive it without reducing the speed of movement; – attacking players should deliver the ball into the limited space without letting the ball leave the «corridor» as fast as possible
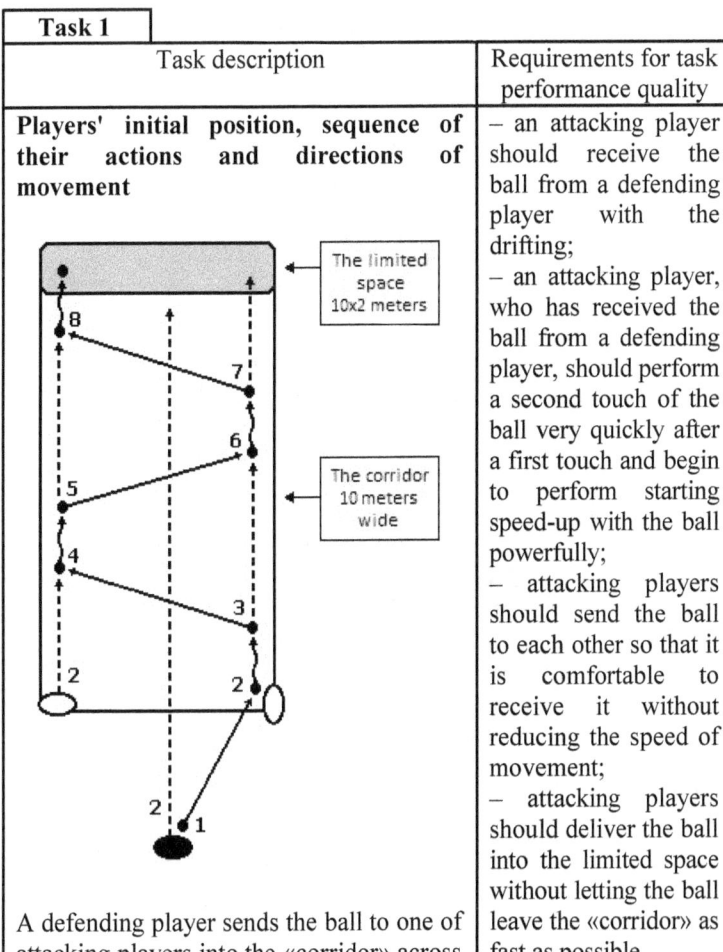	
A defending player sends the ball to one of attacking players into the «corridor» across the pitch surface.	

Task 1 continuation	
Task description	Requirements for task performance quality
An attacking player receives the ball, and attacking players quickly deliver the ball through the «corridor» into the limited space, moving in parallel to each other and **combining pass and dribbling** at short distances in such manner that each attacking player, having received the ball, would perform dribbling at a short distance obligingly. When an attacking player makes his first touch of the ball, a defending player begins to move towards attacking players and tries to prevent them from delivering the ball into the limited space. **Variants:** a) length of the «corridor» is varied; b) one of attacking players performs passes with a first touch obligingly, a second – after dribbling at a short distance; c) one of attacking players performs passes with a second touch obligingly, a second – after dribbling at a short distance. **Note.** A distance at which a defending player is positioned in the initial position from attacking players should be such that he could be close enough to attacking players, beginning the movement when an attacking player touches the ball, but at the same time that attacking players could deliver the ball into the limited space, acting with a maximum speed and precision	

Task 2	
Task description	Requirements for task performance quality
Players' initial position, sequence of their actions and directions of movement 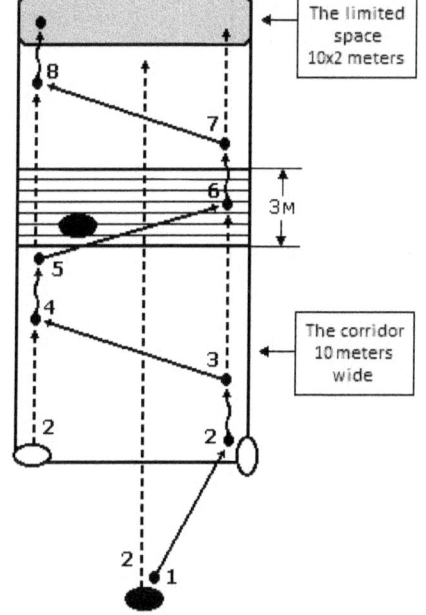	– an attacking player should receive the ball from a defending player with the drifting; – having received the ball from a defending player, an attacking player, should perform a second touch of the ball very quickly after a first touch and begin to perform starting speed-up with the ball powerfully; – attacking players should send the ball to each other so that it is comfortable to receive it without reducing the speed of movement; – attacking players should lower the speed of movement while beating an opponent to a lesser possible extent; – attacking players should deliver the ball into the limited space without letting the ball leave the «corridor» as fast as possible
A defending player, positioned beyond the «corridor», sends the ball to one of attacking players into the «corridor» across the pitch surface. An attacking player receives the ball, and attacking players quickly deliver the ball through the «corridor» into the limited space, moving in parallel to each other and beating a defending player, positioned in the zone crossing the «corridor», on course of movement by means of passes and dribbling.	

Task 2 continuation	
Task description	Requirements for task performance quality
When an attacking player makes his first touch of the ball, a defending player, positioned beyond the «corridor», begins to move towards attacking players and tries to prevent them from delivering the ball into the limited space. A defending player, positioned in the zone crossing the «corridor», tries to prevent attacking players from delivering the ball into the limited space. **Variants:** a) length of the «corridor» is varied; b) on course of movement attacking players consequently beat two defending players, positioned in two zones crossing the «corridor» (points of marking of the zone crossing the «corridor» are varied relative to the initial position of an attacking player (closer-further). **Note.** A distance at which a defending player is positioned in the initial position beyond the «corridor» from attacking players should be such that he could be close enough to attacking players, beginning the movement when an attacking player touches the ball, but at the same time that attacking players could deliver the ball into the limited space, acting with a maximum speed and precision	

Task 3

Task description	Requirements for task performance quality
Players' initial position, sequence of their actions and directions of movement Pitch size: 15 meters wide, 30 meters long. Three zones are marked on the pitch: attacking and defensive 7 meters long each and the middle 16 meters long. The attacking zone is divided into two halves: right and left. Two attacking players, two defending players and a «neutral» player, acting for the attacking team all the time, are positioned in the defensive zone in initial position. 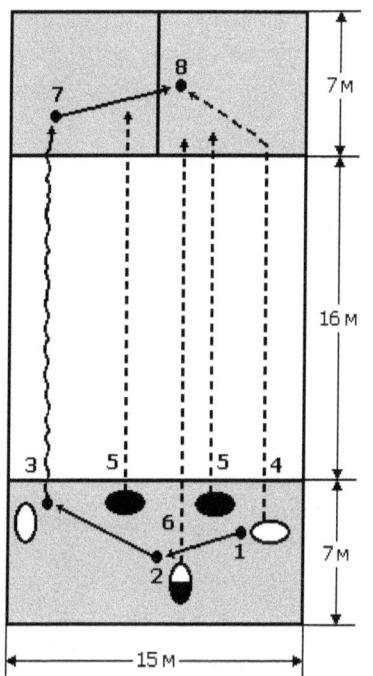	– attacking players should try to create an opportunity to one of their partners to begin to deliver the ball from the defensive to the attacking zone as fast as possible; – an attacking player, delivering the ball from the defensive to the attacking zone, should begin to perform starting speed-up with the ball powerfully; – partners of an attacking player, who has delivered the ball into one of halves of the attacking zone, should try to take most comfortable positions in another half for receiving the ball every time; – an attacking player who has delivered the ball to one of halves of the attacking zone should pass the ball to a partner precisely at foot into another half without a delay

Task 3 continuation	
Task description	Requirements for task performance quality
Players from the attacking team try to beat defending players in the defensive zone, deliver the ball into any half of the attacking zone with dribbling and perform a pass to one of their partners into another half. In case a player from the attacking team comes over the ball in the attacking zone after a pass from a partner, the attacking team gets one point and the right to deliver the ball from the defensive into the attacking zone once again. Defending players try to prevent attacking player from delivering the ball from the defensive into the attacking zone, performing a pass to a partner in the attacking zone and coming over the ball after a pass from a partner. In case defending players tackle the ball or knock it out of the pitch, they get the right to deliver the ball from the defensive into the attacking zone. Attacking and defending players are prohibited from leaving the defensive zone before the ball leaves it. Number of passes by players from the attacking team in the defensive zone is no more than three. Time of possession by an attacking player from the moment of the ball delivery into the attacking zone to the moment of performing a pass to a partner is limited. **Variants:** a) length of the middle zone is varied; b) drill is performed by three attacking players, three defending players and a neutral player, acting for the attacking team all the time, on the pitch 20 meters wide	

Soccer. Training the «game episodes technique», beginning from coming over the ball in open play

Task 4	
Task description	Requirements for task performance quality
Players' initial position, sequence of their actions and directions of movement Pitch size: 12 meters wide, 50 meters long. Three zones are marked on the pitch: the defensive 10 meters long, the middle 25 meters long, attacking 15 meters long. Two attacking players are positioned in the defensive zone, one defending player – on the border of the defensive and the middle zones, second one – in the attacking zone. 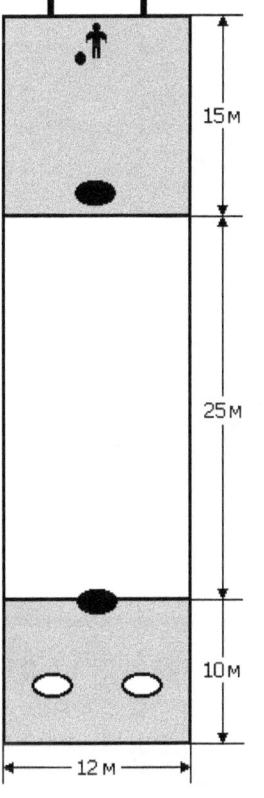	– attacking players should try to deliver the ball into the attacking zone quickly and shoot on goal; – a defending player, positioned of the border of the defensive and the middle zones, should attack a player, who has gained possession of the ball, as fast as possible, forcing him to act amid time and space shortage; – a defending player, positioned in the attacking zone, should actively confront attacking players; – players should perform shots on goal from any, even inconvenient positions; – players should try to use every opportunity to finish off the ball into the net; – while performing shots on goal, players should try to send the ball into the area of the goal, unprotected by the goalkeeper, every time

197

Task 4 continuation	
Task description	Requirements for task performance quality
The goalkeeper sends the ball to one of attacking players with a foot or a hand into the defensive zone with a mounted trajectory. An attacking player receives the ball, and attacking players try to beat a defending player in the defensive zone, deliver the ball into the attacking zone with passes and dribbling and shoot on goal. A defending player, positioned at the border of the defensive and middle zones, firstly tries to steal the ball from attacking players or keep the attack down, acting from the moment when an attacking player firstly touches the ball in the defensive zone, but if attacking players succeed in delivering the ball into the middle zone, he tries to prevent attacking players from delivering the ball into the attacking zone and shooting on goal, acting all over the pitch. A defending player, positioned in the attacking zone, tries to prevent attacking players to deliver the ball into the attacking zone and shooting on goal. Attacking players and a defending player, positioned in the defensive zone, are prohibited from leaving the defensive zone before the ball leaves it. Number of passes by attacking players is no more than two in the defensive zone and no more than two in the attacking zone. The time of the attack is limited from the moment of a first touch of the ball by an attacking player till the moment of shooting on goal. **Variant:** length of the middle zone is varied	

Soccer. Training the «game episodes technique», beginning from coming over the ball in open play

Task 5	
Task description	Requirements for task performance quality
Players' initial position, sequence of their actions and directions of movement	
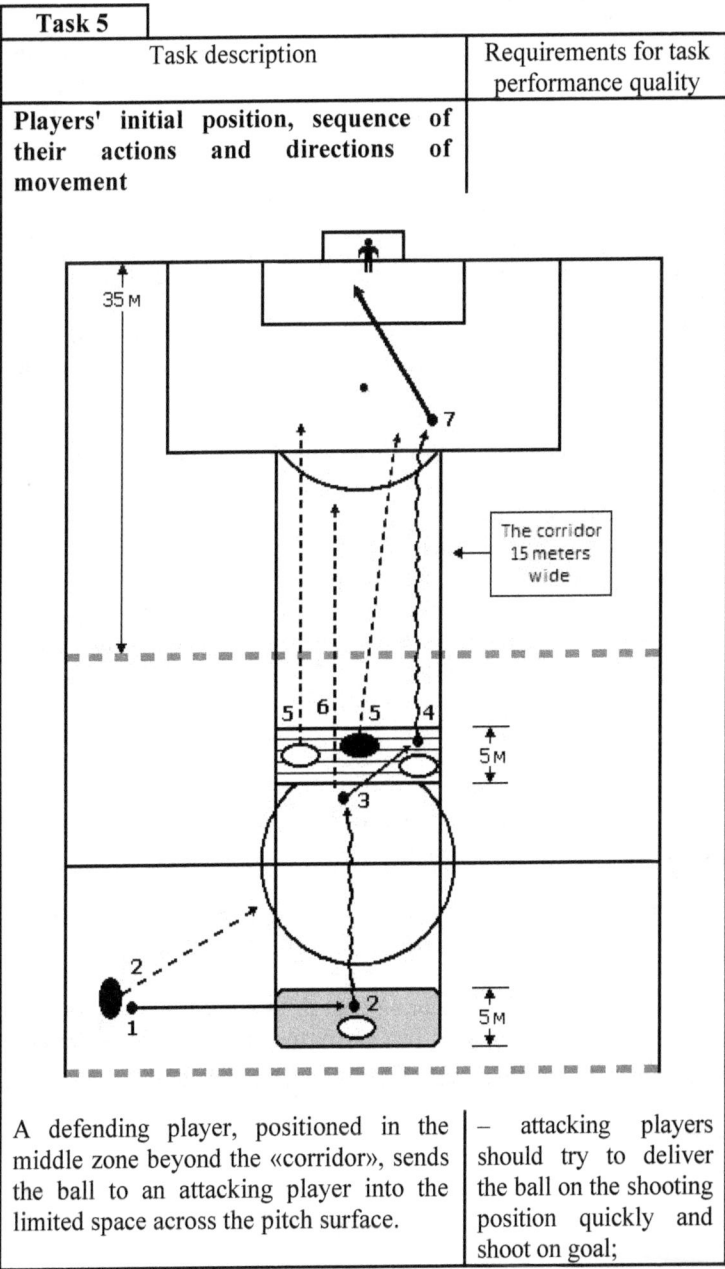 A defending player, positioned in the middle zone beyond the «corridor», sends the ball to an attacking player into the limited space across the pitch surface.	– attacking players should try to deliver the ball on the shooting position quickly and shoot on goal;

Task 5 continuation	
Task description	Requirements for task performance quality
An attacking player receives the ball, begins to move with it through the «corridor» towards the 18-yard box and then tries to quickly deliver the ball through the «corridor» into the 18-yard box with passes and dribbling with two partners and shoot on goal. When an attacking player makes his first touch of the ball, a defending player, positioned in the middle zone beyond the «corridor», begins to move towards attacking players and tries to prevent them from delivering the ball into the 18-yard box and shoot on goal. A defending player, positioned in the zone crossing the «corridor», tries to prevent attacking players from delivering the ball into the 18-yard box and shooting on goal, acting all over the «corridor» from the moment when an attacking player firstly touches the ball. **Offsides are given.** Variants: a) a defending player sends the ball to an attacking player with a bounce off the pitch surface and with a mounted trajectory; b) length of the «corridor» and point of its marking relative to the central lengthwise line of the pitch; c) attacking player can shoot on goal from the outside of the 18-yard box no further than 25 meters from the goal-line	– having received the ball from a defending player, an attacking player should perform a second touch of the ball very quickly after a first touch and begin to perform starting speed-up with the ball powerfully; – attacking players should lower the speed of movement while beating opponents to a lesser possible extent; – attacking players should interact with the ball precisely, without letting it leave the «corridor»; – players should try to use every opportunity to finish off the ball into the net; – while performing shots on goal, players should try to send the ball into the area of the goal, unprotected by the goalkeeper, every time

Soccer. Training the «game episodes technique», beginning from coming over the ball in open play

Task 6	
Task description	Requirements for task performance quality
Players' initial position, sequence of their actions and directions of movement	

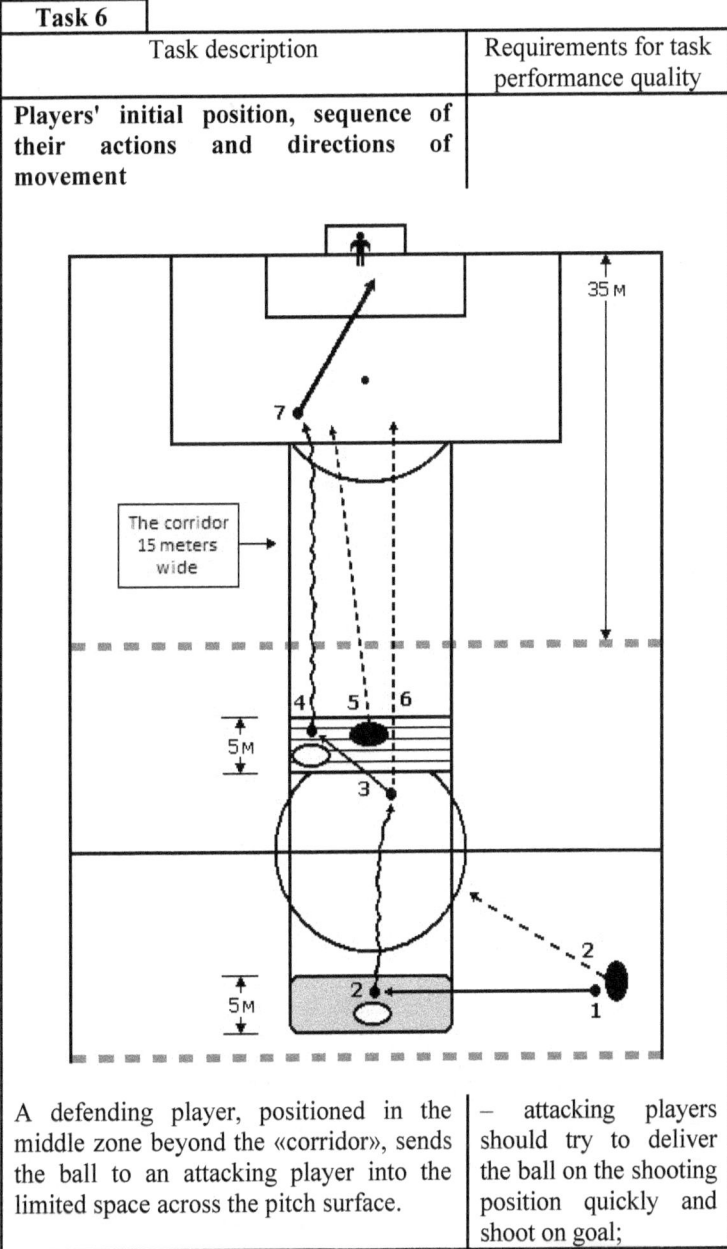

| A defending player, positioned in the middle zone beyond the «corridor», sends the ball to an attacking player into the limited space across the pitch surface. | – attacking players should try to deliver the ball on the shooting position quickly and shoot on goal; |

Task 6 continuation	
Task description	Requirements for task performance quality
An attacking player receives the ball, begins to move with it through the «corridor» towards the 18-yard box and then tries to quickly deliver the ball through the «corridor» into the 18-yard box with passes and dribbling with a partner and shoot on goal. When an attacking player makes his first touch of the ball, a defending player, positioned in the middle zone beyond the «corridor», begins to move towards attacking players and tries to prevent them from delivering the ball into the 18-yard box and shoot on goal. A defending player, positioned in the zone crossing the «corridor», tries to prevent attacking players from delivering the ball into the 18-yard box and shooting on goal, acting all over the «corridor» from the moment when an attacking player firstly touches the ball. **Offsides are given.** Variants: a) a defending player sends the ball to an attacking player with a bounce off the pitch surface and with a mounted trajectory; b) length of the «corridor» and point of its marking relative to the central lengthwise line of the pitch; c) attacking player can shoot on goal from the outside of the 18-yard box no further than 25 meters from the goal-line	– having received the ball from a defending player, an attacking player should perform a second touch of the ball very quickly after a first touch and begin to perform starting speed-up with the ball powerfully; – attacking players should lower the speed of movement while beating opponents to a lesser possible extent; – attacking players should interact with the ball precisely, without letting it leave the «corridor»; – players should try to use every opportunity to finish off the ball into the net; – while performing shots on goal, players should try to send the ball into the area of the goal, unprotected by the goalkeeper, every time

Task 7

Task description	Requirements for task performance quality
Players' initial position, sequence of their actions and directions of movement	

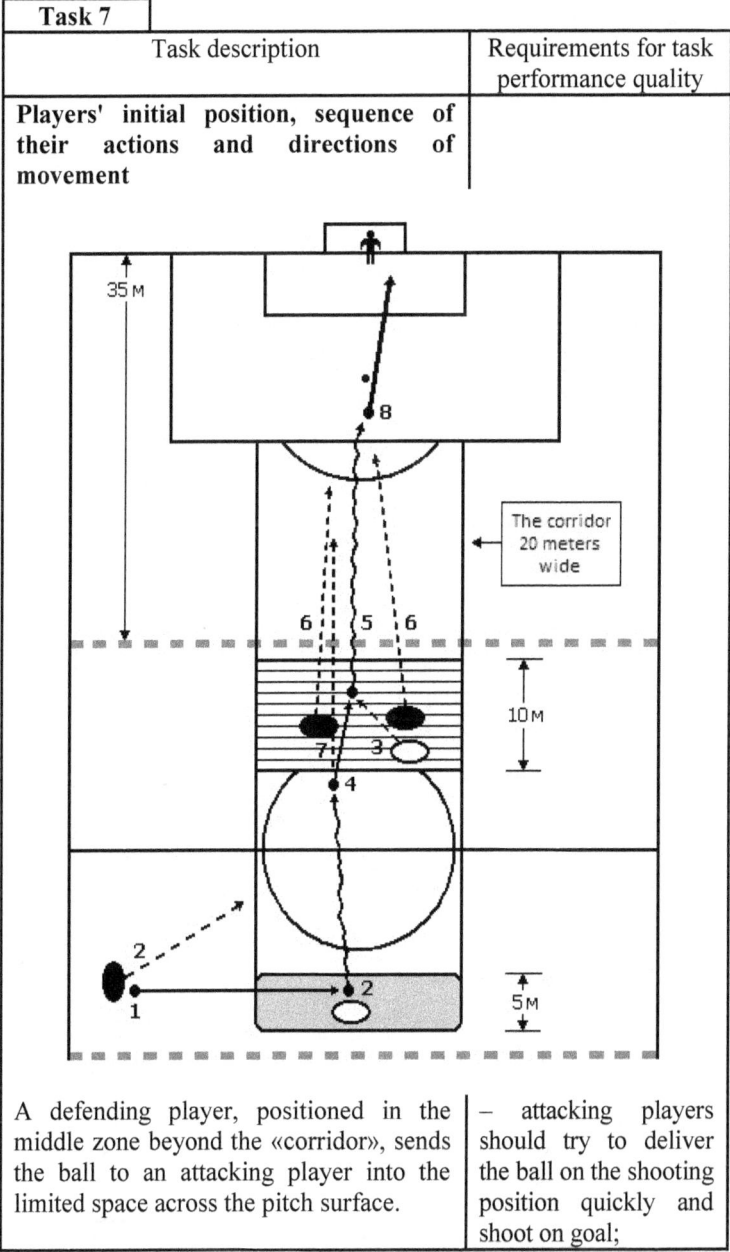

A defending player, positioned in the middle zone beyond the «corridor», sends the ball to an attacking player into the limited space across the pitch surface.	− attacking players should try to deliver the ball on the shooting position quickly and shoot on goal;

Task 7 continuation	
Task description	Requirements for task performance quality
An attacking player receives the ball, begins to move with it through the «corridor» towards the 18-yard box and then tries to quickly deliver the ball through the «corridor» into the 18-yard box with passes and dribbling with a partner and shoot on goal. When an attacking player makes his first touch of the ball, a defending player, positioned in the middle zone beyond the «corridor», begins to move towards attacking players and tries to prevent them from delivering the ball into the 18-yard box and shoot on goal. Defending players, positioned in the zone crossing the «corridor», try to prevent attacking players from delivering the ball into the 18-yard box and shooting on goal, acting all over the «corridor» from the moment when an attacking player firstly touches the ball. **Offsides are given.** Variants: a) a defending player sends the ball to an attacking player with a bounce off the pitch surface and on air low-level; b) length of the «corridor» and point of its marking relative to the central lengthwise line of the pitch; c) attacking player can shoot on goal from the outside of the 18-yard box no further than 25 meters from the goal-line	– having received the ball from a defending player, an attacking player should perform a second touch of the ball very quickly after a first touch and begin to perform starting speed-up with the ball powerfully; – attacking players should lower the speed of movement while beating opponents to a lesser possible extent; – attacking players should interact with the ball precisely, without letting it leave the «corridor»; – players should try to use every opportunity to finish off the ball into the net; – while performing shots on goal, players should try to send the ball into the area of the goal, unprotected by the goalkeeper, every time

Soccer. Training the «game episodes technique», beginning from coming over the ball in open play

Drills in which space is covered by means of passes at a long distance

Task 1	
Task description	Requirements for task performance quality
Players' initial position, sequence of their actions and directions of movement	

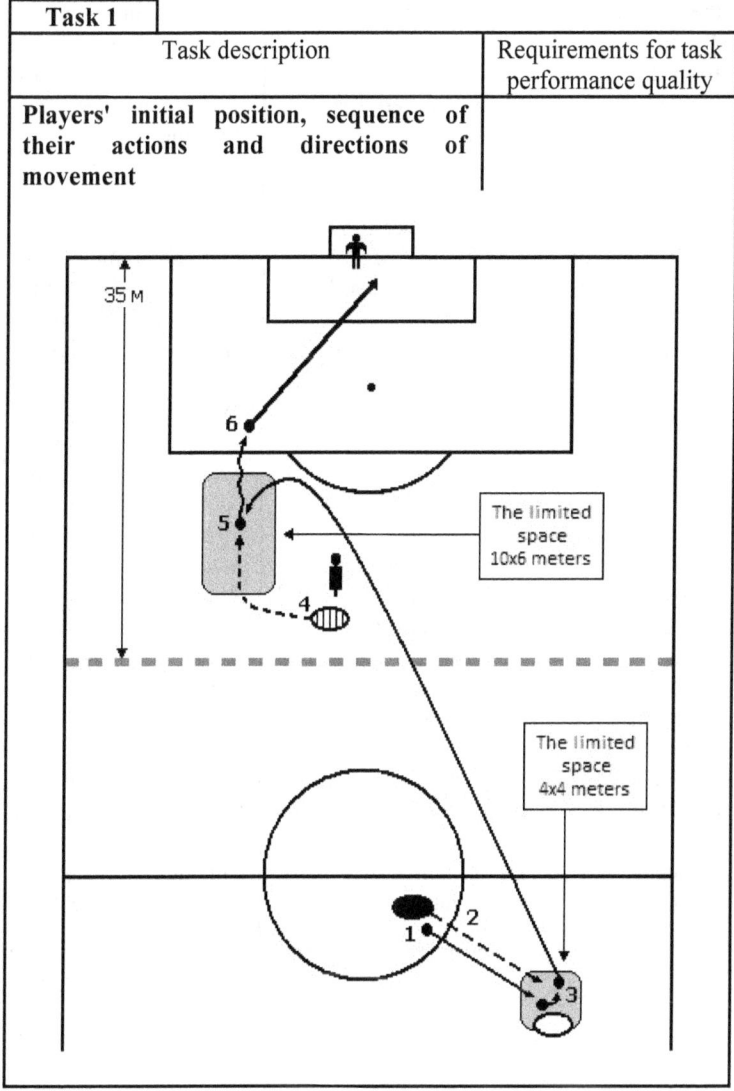

205

Task 1 continuation	
Task description	Requirements for task performance quality
A defending player sends the ball to an attacking player into the limited space in the middle zone across the pitch surface. An attacking player receives the ball and from the limited space sends it at an angle to the goal-line into the limited space at the corner of the 18-yard box above the mannequine, designating a defending player. A partner of an attacking player moves in an arc into the limited space, receives the ball, moves with it into the 18-yard box and shoots on goal. Having performed a pass, a defending player begins to move towards an attacking player and tries to prevent him from performing a pass. **Variant:** a) a defending player sends the ball to an attacking player with a bounce off the pitch surface and on air low-level; b) points of marking of limited spaces and players' initial position are varied. **Note.** A distance at which a defending player is positioned in the initial position from an attacking player should be such that he could come up with an attacking player when the latter performs a pass, beginning the movement after performing a pass, but at the same time that an attacking player could perform a pass, acting with a maximum speed and precision	– a defending player should send the ball to an attacking player precisely at foot; – while preparing to perform a pass, an attacking player should act with the ball with a maximum speed; – an attacking player should send the ball to his partner precisely into the limited space with the lowest possible trajectory, yet so that it flew above a mannequin designating a defending player; – a partner of an attacking player should begin to move into the limited space timely relative to the moment of the pass performing by an attacking player; – a partner of an attacking player should come over the ball without reducing the speed of movement

Soccer. Training the «game episodes technique», beginning from coming over the ball in open play

Task 2	
Task description	Requirements for task performance quality
Players' initial position, sequence of their actions and directions of movement	

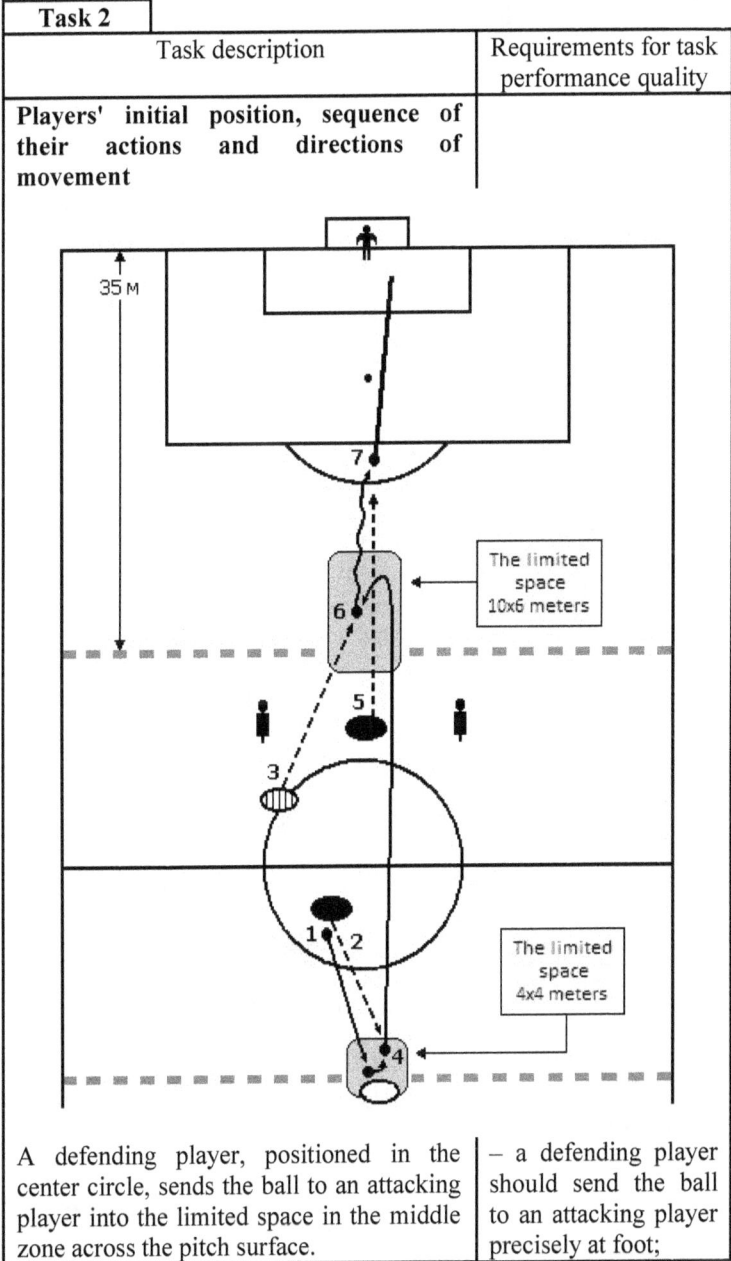

A defending player, positioned in the center circle, sends the ball to an attacking player into the limited space in the middle zone across the pitch surface.	– a defending player should send the ball to an attacking player precisely at foot;

Task 2 continuation	
Task description	Requirements for task performance quality
An attacking player receives the ball and from limited space sends it perpendicularly to the goal-line into the limited space in the attacking zone above a defending player, positioned at the center circle. A partner of an attacking player moves on the straight into the limited space, receives the ball, moves with it into the 18-yard box and shoots on goal. Having performed a pass, a defending player, positioned in the center circle, begins to move towards an attacking player and tries to prevent him from performing a pass. A defending player, positioned at the center circle, tries to prevent a partner of an attacking player from shooting on goal, beginning to act when the latter appears directly close to him. **Variant:** a) a defending player sends the ball to an attacking player with a bounce off the pitch surface and on air low-level; b) points of marking of limited spaces and players' initial position are varied. **Note.** A distance at which a defending player is positioned in the initial position in the center circle from an attacking player should be such that he could come up with an attacking player when the latter performs a pass, beginning the movement after performing a pass, but at the same time that an attacking player could perform a pass, acting with a maximum speed and precision	– while preparing to perform a pass, an attacking player should act with the ball with a maximum speed; – an attacking player should send the ball to his partner precisely into the limited space with the lowest possible trajectory, yet so that it flew above a defending player; – a partner of an attacking player should begin to move into the limited space timely relative to the moment of the pass performing by an attacking player; – a partner of an attacking player should come over the ball without reducing the speed of movement; – a partner of an attacking player, performing shots on goal, should try to send the ball on target every time

Task 3

Task description	Requirements for task performance quality
Players' initial position, sequence of their actions and directions of movement 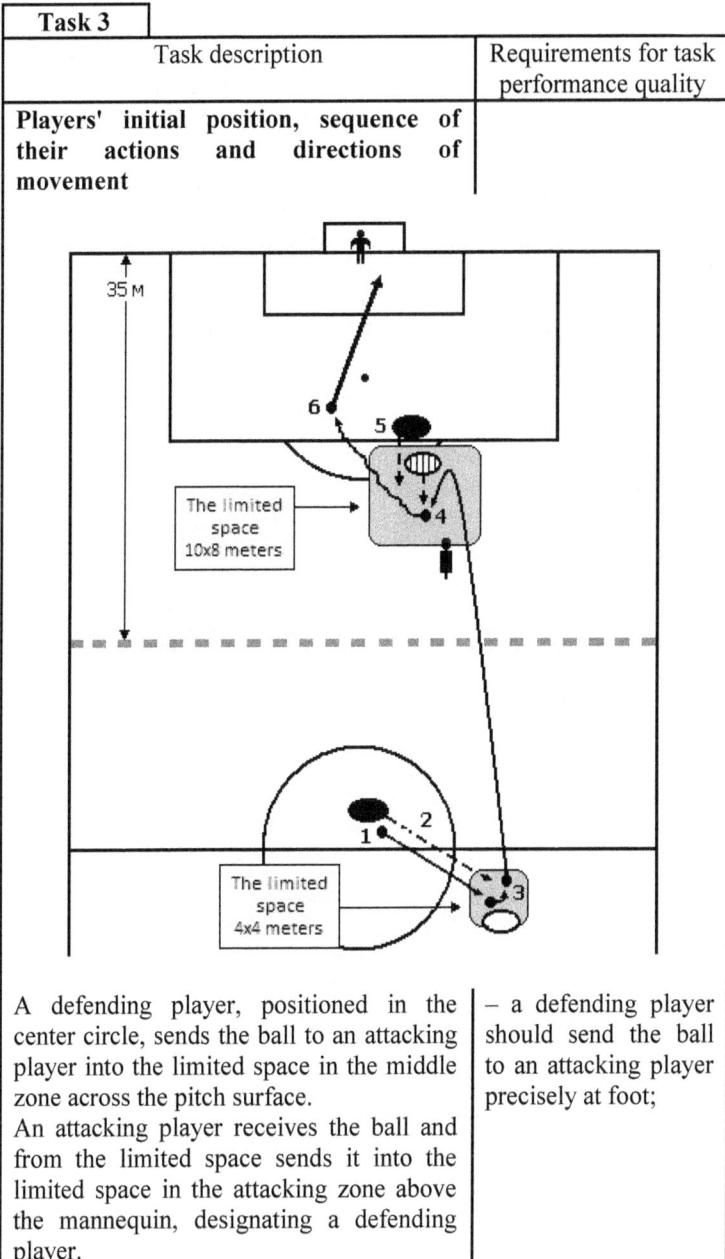	– a defending player should send the ball to an attacking player precisely at foot;
A defending player, positioned in the center circle, sends the ball to an attacking player into the limited space in the middle zone across the pitch surface. An attacking player receives the ball and from the limited space sends it into the limited space in the attacking zone above the mannequin, designating a defending player.	

Task 3 continuation	
Task description	Requirements for task performance quality
A partner of an attacking player receives the ball in the limited space back to the opponents' goal, quickly moves into the 18-yard box, beating a defending player on course of movement, and shoots on goal. Having performed a pass, a defending player, positioned in the center circle, begins to move towards an attacking player and tries to prevent him from performing a pass. A defending player, positioned in the 18-yard box, tries to prevent a partner of an attacking player from shooting on goal, beginning to act when an attacking player firstly touches the ball. **Variant:** a) a defending player sends the ball to an attacking player with a bounce off the pitch surface and on air low-level; b) points of marking of limited spaces and players' initial position are varied. **Note.** A distance at which a defending player is positioned in the initial position in the center circle from an attacking player should be such that he could come up with an attacking player when the latter performs a pass, beginning the movement after performing a pass, but at the same time that an attacking player could perform a pass, acting with a maximum speed and precision	– while preparing to perform a pass, an attacking player should act with the ball with a maximum speed; – an attacking player should send the ball to his partner precisely into the limited space with the lowest possible trajectory, yet so that it flew above a mannequin designnating a defending player; – a partner of an attacking player should quickly perform a twist, beating of an opponent and movement into the 18-yard box without letting the ball leave the 18-yard box – while performing shots on goal, a partner of an attacking player should try to send the ball into the area of the goal, unprotected by the goalkeeper, every time

Soccer. Training the «game episodes technique», beginning from coming over the ball in open play

Task 4		
	Task description	Requirements for task performance quality
	Two on two play with two «neutral» players acting for the attacking team all the time providing one player acting all the time in the defensive zone, another – in the attacking zone, one «neutral» in the defensive zone all the time and another – in the attacking zone. Pitch size: 30 meters wide, 60 meters long. Three zones are marked on the pitch: the attacking, the defensive and the middle 20 meters long each. In each one player acts in his team defensive zone, and another – in the attacking zone all the time. One «neutral» player acting in the defensive area, and another – in the attacking zone all the time. Players are prohibited from moving from zone to zone. Goalkeepers put the ball into play to their team defensive zone after catching it or when it crosses the goal-line and sidelines. Players from the attacking team, positioned in the defensive zone, try to beat one player from the defending team and pass the ball to partners in the attacking zone with a mounted trajectory above the middle zone. Players from the attacking team, positioned in the attacking zone, try to beat a player from the defending team and shoot on goal. Players from the attacking zone, positioned in the attacking zone, are prohibited from playing one and two touches for receiving the ball in the defensive zone.	– goalkeepers should put the ball into play without a delay; – a player from the defending team acting in the opponents' defensive zone should attack a rival player to whom the ball is passed as quick as possible, forcing him to act amid time and space shortage; – players from the attacking team, positioned in the attacking zones, should try to take most comfortable positions for receiving the ball from the defensive zone every time; – players from the attacking team should timely and precisely perform passes to partners into the attacking zone, sending the ball with a mounted trajectory directly to a player or on his way;

Task 4 continuation	
Task description	Requirements for task performance quality
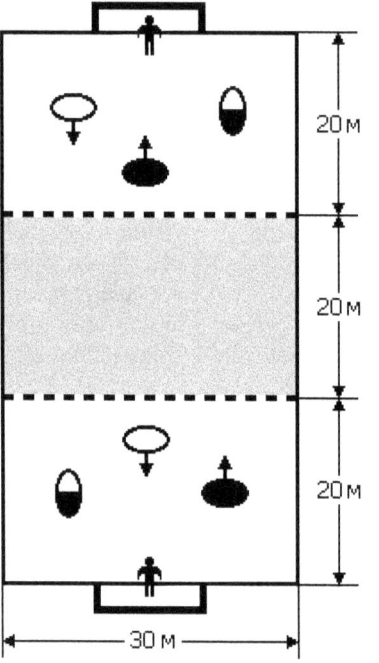	– players from the attacking team, positioned in the attacking zone, should powerfully switch into the game after coming over the ball; – while performing shots on goal, players should try to send the ball into the area of the goal, unprotected by the goalkeeper, every time
Players from the attacking team, positioned in the defensive zone, are prohibited to pass the ball to each other. Number of passes by players from the attacking team, positioned in the attacking zone, during the attack is no more than one. Corners are not awarded. Offsides are not given. Play time in one repeat – 5 minutes. **Variants:** length of the middle zone is varied	

Soccer. Training the «game episodes technique», beginning from coming over the ball in open play

For notes

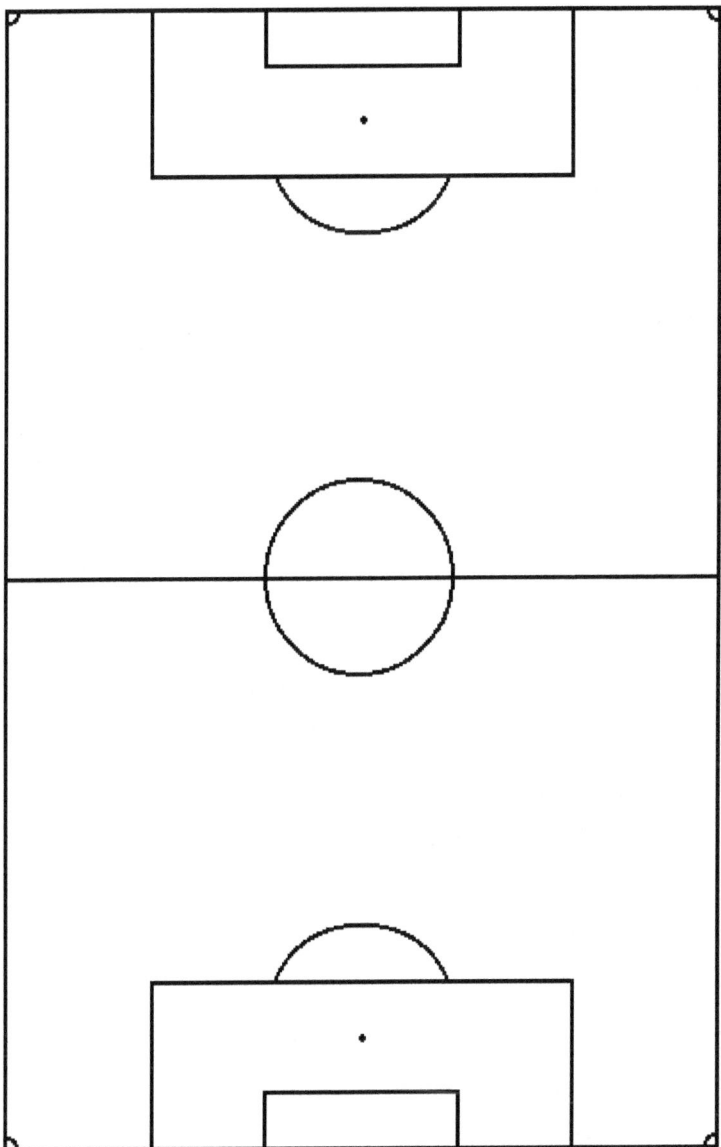

AFTERWORD

First. The analysis of condition and specificity of performance of actions with the ball by high class players in various areas of the pitch in competitive matches allows to mark out the «game episodes technique»:
– inside the 18-yard box;
– in the attacking zone (no further than 35 meters from the defending team's goal-line);
– in the defensive and middle zones (no closer than 35 meters from the defending team's goal-line).

Second. Considering there are three kinds of the «game episodes technique», beginning with players coming over the ball in play, the improvement of technical skills by players suggests training the technique of actions with the ball, typical for play situations in the 18-yard box, the attacking, middle and defensive zones.

Third. There should be various degree of premeditation and improvisation of players' actions in drills for perfection of the «game episodes technique», beginning from coming over the ball in open play, as in episodes of competitive matches. This explains the need for applying those kind of drills, during performance of with players' actions with the ball:
– begin and finish regularly;
– begin regularly and finish variatively;
– begin variatively and finish variatively.

Fourth. It is important that players, training principal actions in a drill, should not possess the ball before the drill beginning, but begin their actions exactly with the reception of the ball even while performing regularly beginning drills. This is due to the fact that in these cases the assessment of situation and variants of interaction with partner goes differently, and therefore the structure of their movements while performing initial actions with the ball essentially differs.

Fifth. The efficiency of trainings for improving the play technique is due to the quality of performance of drills by players, which suggests the quickness of players' taking proper decision in the beginning of attacking actions and speed and precision of actions with the ball. Depending on which area of the pitch attacking actions begin in, the priority should be placed on the quickness and precision of the attack beginning or on the quickness and precision of its undergoing.

It is necessary to involve a small number of players for performance of a large amount of repeats of actions with the ball in drills.

Sixth. Drills for perfection of the «game episodes technique», beginning with coming over the ball in open play, may be applied not only in professional teams, but also in youth teams. Many of these drills were tested in youth soccer, and, as shown by experience, are quite teachable for young soccer players, at least from 11 y.o. and on.

Seventh. When using drills for perfection of the «game episodes technique», beginning with coming over the ball in open play, in youth soccer, it is necessary to adjust organization of these drills in each specific case depending on age and level of training of young players to ensure the potential and quality of task performance by players.

Conditions of drills may notably vary in the context of distance of passes and movements with the ball, and the size of the limited space for actions with the ball.

BIBLIOGRAPHY

Бесков К.И. Игровой метод в действии / К.И. Бесков // Футбол: ежегодник 1981. – М.: Физкультура и спорт, 1981. – С. 9-16.

Бидзински М. Искусство первого касания мяча. Как подготовить техничного футболиста (пер. с англ. А.В. Зубковой) / М. Бидзински. – М., Фонд «Национальная академия футбола»; Нижний Новгород, 2009. – 146 с.

Бил М. 140 игровых упражнений. Игра в численном неравенстве и завершение атаки (пер. с англ. А.В. Зубковой) / М. Бил. – М., Фонд «Национальная академия футбола»; Нижний Новгород, РА «Квартал», 2009. – 160 с.

Блащак И.М. Точность ударов по воротам в соревнованиях и тренировках футболистов и факторы, ее определяющие: автореф. дис. ... канд. пед. наук / И.М. Блащак; ГЦОЛИФК. – М., 1991. – 22 с.

Варюшин В.В. Игровые упражнения в тренировке взаимодействия футболистов: метод. разработки для слушателей ВШТ, факультета повышения квалификации ГЦОЛИФКа / В.В. Варюшин. – М., ГЦОЛИФК, 1989. – 77 с.

Герасименко А.П., Кашигин А.И., Князев В.Д. Изучение игровых ситуаций, отражающих связь с игровой деятельностью футболиста / А.П. Герасименко, А.И. Кашигин, В.Д. Князев // В книге: Вопросы управления подготовкой юных спортсменов. – Волгоград, 1979. – С. 25-28.

Голденко Г.А. Индивидуальные программы технико-тактической подготовки футболистов высокой квалификации с учетом особенностей соревновательной деятельности: дис. ... канд. пед. наук / Г.А. Голденко; ВНИИФК. – М., 1984. – 217 с.

Голомазов С., Чирва Б. Упражнения со стандартным началом и стандартным завершением для совершенствования «техники эпизодов игры» в штрафной площади / С. Голомазов, Б. Чирва // Теория и практика футбола – 2001. – № 2. – С. 23-29.

Голомазов С., Чирва Б. Методология построения упражнений для совершенствования техники атакующих действий в средней зоне и зоне обороны / С. Голомазов, Б. Чирва // Теория и практика футбола. – 2001. – № 4. – С. 26-28.

Голомазов С.В., Чирва Б.Г. Футбол. Методика тренировки техники игры головой / С.В. Голомазов, Б.Г. Чирва – М.: ТВТ Дивизион, 2006. – 112 с.

Губа В.П., Лексаков А.В. Теория и методика футбола: учебник / В.П. Губа, А.В. Лексаков. – М.: Советский спорт, 2013. – 536 с.

Искусство подготовки высококлассных футболистов: научно-методическое пособие / Под ред. Н.М. Люкшинова. – М.: Советский спорт, 2003. – 416 с.

Качани Л., Горский Л. Тренировка футболистов (пер. со словацкого) / Л. Качани, Л. Горский. – Братислава: Спорт, 1984. – 288 с.

Ковтученко А.И. Некоторые статистические закономерности в футболе / А.И. Ковтученко // Теория и практика физической культуры. – 1975. – № 1. – С. 20-22.

Люкшинов Н.М., Шамардин В.Н. Несоответствие игры и тренировки / Н.М. Люкшинов, В.Н. Шамардин // Еженедельник «Футбол-Хоккей». – 1978. – № 2. – С. 8.

Монаков Г.В. Техническая подготовка футболистов. Методика и планирование / Г.В. Монаков. – Псков, 2000. – 127 с.

Никитин Д.В. Оптимизация планирования специализированных упражнений в учебно-тренировочном процессе высококвалифицированных футболистов: автореф. дис. ... канд. пед. наук / Д.В. Никитин; ВГАФК. – Волгоград, 1998. – 23 с.

Осташев П.В. Совершенствование методики технической подготовки футболистов: автореф. дис. ... канд. пед. наук / П.В. Осташев; ГДОИФК им. П.Ф. Лесгафта. – Л., 1967. – 16 с.

Плон Б. Новая школа в футбольной тренировке / Б. Плон. – М.: Терра-Спорт, 2003. – 240 с.

Полишкис М.С., Выжгин В.А., Сагасти Р.Р. Технико-тактическая подготовка квалифицированных футболистов: учебное пособие для слушателей ВШТ / М.С. Полишкис, В.А. Выжгин, Р.Р. Сагасти. – М., 1989. – 88 с.

Попов А.В. Интенсификация двигательного совершенства техники игры / А.В. Попов // Футбол: Ежегодник 1980. – М.: Физкультура и спорт, 1980. – С. 47-51.

Попов А.В. Совершенствование технической подготовки футболистов с учетом типов ударных движений и условий игровой деятельности: автореф. дис. ... канд. пед. наук / А.В. Попов; КГИФК. – Киев, 1981. – 24 с.

Рымашевский Г.А. Экспериментальное обоснование некоторых путей повышения надежности выполнения технико-тактических действий футболистами высокой квалификации: автореф. дис. ... канд. пед. наук / Г.А. Рымашевский; ВНИИФК. – М., 1978. – 22 с.

Цирик Б. Ворота в центре / Б. Цирик // Еженедельник «Футбол-Хоккей». – 1973. – № 25. – С. 10-11.

Чанади А. Футбол. Техника / А. Чанади. – М.: Физкультура и спорт, 1978. – 253 с.

Чирва Б. Методология построения упражнений для совершенствования «техники эпизодов игры» в зоне атаки / Б. Чирва // Теория и практика футбола. – 2001. – № 3. – С. 34-36.

Чирва Б.Г. Аналитические закономерности игры в футбол как основа для выбора тактики игры и построения технико-тактической подготовки квалифицированных футболистов / Б.Г. Чирва // Теория и практика физической культуры. – 2006. – № 7. – С. 28-29.

Чирва Б.Г. Футбол. Методика совершенствования «техники эпизодов игры» / Б.Г. Чирва. – М.: ТВТ Дивизион, 2006. – 112 с.

Чирва Б.Г. Основные положения переноса тренированности в быстроте и точности действий с мячом в футболе / Б.Г. Чирва // Физическая культура: воспитание, образование, тренировка. – 2008. – № 3. – С. 30-32.

Чирва Б.Г. Футбол. Игровые упражнения при сближенных воротах для тренировки техники игры / Б.Г. Чирва. – М.: ТВТ Дивизион, 2008. – 120 с.

Чирва Б.Г. Футбол. Первенство Европы 2008 г.: удары по воротам: метод. разработки для тренеров. Выпуск 31 / Б.Г. Чирва. – М., РГУФКСиТ, 2009. – 56 с.

Чирва Б.Г., Козлов В.С. Футбол. Перемещения полевых игроков с мячом в играх Первенства Европы 2008 г.: метод. разработки для тренеров. Выпуск 34 / Б.Г. Чирва, В.С. Козлов. – М., РГУФКСиТ, 2011. – 52 с.

Чирва Б.Г. Футбол. Концепция технической и тактической подготовки футболистов. – 2-е изд., перераб. и доп. / Б.Г. Чирва. – М.: ТВТ Дивизион, 2015. – 352 с.

Яромко В.И., Ковалев В.В. Анализ условий выполнения ударов в футболе / В.И. Яромко, В.В. Ковалев // В сборнике: Вопросы теории и практики физ. культуры и спорта. – Минск: Полымя, 1990. – С. 132-135.

www.ingramcontent.com/pod-product-compliance
Lightning Source LLC
Chambersburg PA
CBHW071702090426
42738CB00009B/1633